Owned

Marie Campbell

JJ Books

Copyright © [Year of First Publication] by [Author or Pen Name]

All rights reserved.

No portion of this book may be reproduced in any form without written permission from the publisher or author, except as permitted by U.S. copyright law.

Contents

1. Creating the Twist 1
2. The Ingredients that Made the Cake 9
3. Moving Day 14
4. The Doorway to a Whole New World 20
5. The Wall 26
6. Rebuilding 32
7. A Storm is Brewing 37
8. An Old Foot in a New Shoe 41
9. A Tumultuous Relationship 48
10. A Fast Exit onto a New Level 55
11. The Curtain 58
12. Torn 62
13. The Cold, the Street and the Ugly 67
14. A Doorway Through to Another Land 71
15. Kidnapped 75

16.	Inside-out	81
17.	Fizz	86
18.	Paranoia and Delivery	90
19.	Purchased	96
20.	Greener Grass Still Needs Mowing	101
21.	Paying Up	107
22.	King's Table	113
23.	Wearing Shoes of Peace	118
24.	Real Life	124
25.	Quakes in the Soul	129
26.	Splitting	133
27.	The Trapdoor	137
28.	Train Wreck	144
29.	The Silent Night	150
30.	Manic	157
Epilogue		163
Acknowledgements		165

1

Creating the Twist

Do you ever remember, as a child, looking at adults and thinking that they have it easy? No one tells them what to do.

When I was a child, I watched a woman walking down the street; carefree, thin, wild hair; probably a working girl. That's freedom, I thought to myself. An adult could live as wild as they wanted, without rules or expectations. They were lucky, because they could choose whatever they wanted. I couldn't wait to grow up!

I daydreamed a lot, imagining myself in a different world, picked up and taken away by a rich and famous movie star. I'd have whatever I wanted, free from the daily grind of school, the pressure to maintain friendships, and, most of all, I would be away from my parents.

In 1985, I was born in a hospital looking perfect. Two days later I turned blue, and the doctors rushed me off. They discovered I was very sick. I had holes in my heart, all the way down the middle heart wall. Blood from my heart chambers was leaking into the other chambers. They diagnosed me with congenital heart disease.

I had my first major heart operation at a week old. Instead of bonding with my mother, I spent the first months of my life in an incubator, hooked up to machines. They transferred me to another city where Mum couldn't touch me or nurture me.

My brother was 2 years old when I was born and had to be looked after by family while my parents stayed with me in the hospital. Mum and Dad were with me in the hospital for the first two weeks, then they would visit me once a week on the weekends.

My parents had been easy-going, peaceful people, attending church and enjoying a nice married life. When I was born, my dad didn't connect with the reality that I was a sick and dying baby until six weeks after my birth. He seemed to think I was fine and would be home soon. He buried himself in his work and left most of the healthcare to Mum. Meanwhile, Mum had to carry the load of knowing her daughter could die.

Her little boy was acting out at home, and her husband was distant from reality. She explained, later in life, that it was easier for her not to form too much of an attachment with me in the hospital, in case I died. She was now supporting Dad, who had finally faced that reality and was struggling to cope, as well as a two-year-old son whose behaviour was hyperactive and unsettled.

My life over the next four years comprised hospital visits, doctors probing, long stays in the children's ward and then, at four years old, another major heart surgery.

My earliest memory is of doctors trying to hold me down to put an oxygen mask on me. I remember thinking it tasted funny, and screaming, trying to get them away. I felt absolute terror. Perhaps that was the first time I felt out of control of my own body. I was continuously pumped with medications and drugs, separated for long periods from my family and constantly having my personal space encroached on.

Sometimes I enjoyed the attention of being poked and prodded. People worried and fussed over me and I interpreted that as love. Other times, I felt embarrassed and exposed.

I couldn't make sense of these feelings, so I would pretend I was an actress, being paid not to cry. Doctors would come in and assess me. If I was scared or feeling exposed, I would just switch into 'actress' mode and bite my tongue, telling myself I was an actress on a set in Hollywood, being paid to be brave.

They gave me heavy doses of strong medication as I grew up. I look back now and wonder what effect the drugs had on my chemical balance, and the unfolding addictions of the years to come.

As I grew, my mother and I had a hard time bonding and would fight frequently. I would act out for attention and she would respond with stress.

My frequent visits to hospital became more and more spread apart as I started going to school. School was a whole new world. It wasn't like a hospital. The level of care was not as intense. The children were often fickle, making fun of me or just excluding me because I had freckles or couldn't run as fast as them. I was always relieved when we changed school.

We changed schools for various reasons. My brother and I moved schools three times before I was seven. Again, fantasy would be my saviour as I would come up with a new personality; maybe laugh differently, not talk as much, or be the class clown. I would try these new sides of myself at different schools to protect myself from getting hurt again or to avoid possible rejection.

I remember the trauma of going to new schools frequently. Would I make a friend? What if I did and then I had to leave? What if no one liked me and I had to stay? One day I could have a good set of friends and for some reason the next day they would exclude me. I hated it.

That's a normal experience for a lot of kids. However, with the lack of bonding I had with my mother, it felt like my whole world was constantly on shaky ground. I relied on the techniques I had learned in the hospital to get me through my early school years. Often when we had to move schools suddenly and start at a new one, I would employ that same strategy; I was an actress, and I was being paid not to cry.

At my second school, a teacher made me stand up in front of the class to introduce me, when I was about five and a half years old. When the teacher heard my name, she encouraged the class to sing me a welcoming song with my name as the feature of the song. I was highly embarrassed, suddenly faced with a bunch of strange kids laughing at my name being in a song. I started to cry and asked them to stop singing. The children thought this was even funnier, and the teacher let it continue.

I hated that school; I was teased frequently because the children had found a song with my name in it and continued to berate me during play time. I remember feeling sad and not fitting in. I didn't have any friends there and spent my play and lunch times in the cloak bay or reading a book in the library. My older brother went to the same school but was never around to play with. I remember seeing him get scolded by a teacher and marched out of his classroom. He and I hardly saw each other at school because he was always in trouble.

During my sick years, relatives looked after my brother for periods of time. Looking back, I wonder if, as a kid, he couldn't understand this, but saw me as the reason behind his separation from the family.

My sister was born in 1990. I couldn't make sense of having a baby in the house. Watching my parents love on her, especially my mother, brought me a lot of confusion because I hadn't experienced that. My mother found it difficult to bond with me because of the barriers of hospital, but she never gave up praying and fighting for me.

I wasn't too fond of my sister as a baby, but I found it funny watching her crawl around the house. To shut her up one day, I tried to fill her cot with toys, including my heavy roller skates!

As she grew up and began talking and walking, she proved of some value to my life because suddenly I had a little friend. She and I would play fantasy games with our dolls. I had a lamb-chop woollen puppet as my doll; I was never into Barbie's. Mum or Dad would build us dollhouses out of cardboard boxes as we didn't have money for a real one. I would take my puppet to the beach, riding my bike, and sometimes I would pack him in my school bag. Knowing he was there was of immense comfort to me. I named him Billy-Joe.

Billy-Joe, aside from my sister, became my best friend. I had a strong love for him and thought he had a spirit and was real. My brother would tease me by putting him in the freezer, or telling me he'd put him in the rubbish and point to the rubbish truck going down the road. One time I came home, and he had hung him from a noose in the house. To me, this fantasy toy was real; he was my son and I cared for him. I enjoyed controlling the life of my puppet. Sometimes, for reasons I couldn't explain, I would orchestrate harm to him, expressing the inward turmoil I often experienced and could never make sense of. I would cut his arms and think he had self-harm problems, or I would cut his hair, and then, because he was woollen, he would unravel. I would take him to my dad and Dad would knit him back together again.

Dad and I were close, growing up. It always left me wondering if Mum ever loved me or could love me. I thought she was the mean one, and Dad was the hero.

It may have looked that way from the outside, but I didn't know how broken and stressed Mum was, and how much family shit she was holding together. I was around ten or eleven when Dad explained that, as a baby, she separated herself from loving me too much in case I died. Mum was just trying to cope with her own world.

My first best friend was from a primary school that I ended up going to twice. Her name was Julie-Anne. She had long, blonde hair and scruffy clothes, but beautiful blue eyes that were always up to mischief. She and I would get into trouble at school, teasing boys and running around like rat bags. Often my older brother was the target of our games. Her mum had problems, but at that age I didn't understand what or why. I just knew when we went to her place her mum was always dark, quiet, drinking and smoking.

One day I was at her place and her mum didn't come home. It was strange, so we called my parents. They came and collected me and her grandmother came over for her. The next morning Mum and Dad woke me up, which was unusual; I knew something was wrong. They told me her mum had committed suicide on the train tracks behind her house. That's why she never came home that day! I was so deeply sad.

I went off to school but my best friend had gone. I couldn't understand what had happened, but my heart broke for her, knowing her mum had gone. Julie-Anne wouldn't be coming back, I was told. She'd gone to live with her dad and was going to a different school.

I remember going into class. I was a bit late, and the whole class was sitting on the mat. They had just been told. Everyone was staring at me because I was her best friend and we sat on the mat together every day. I didn't know where to sit anymore. I remember sitting down with an ache inside of me and the reality of now not knowing who to sit with. My best friend wouldn't be coming back. Not only was I now alone, because she and I had often teased the other kids and played by ourselves, but now she also was somewhere sad and alone, and without a mummy.

By the time I got to high school, I had developed techniques for playing with the kids in the neighbourhood. I was always sharing, getting creative, and often thought of ways to make money, even as a kid. One time I sold chocolate muffins for $2 each and bought myself a tent; I wanted to be independent and live in the backyard. By around the age of twelve, I had pitched the tent, packed a chilli-bin and was now living outside.

I wasn't always honest about making money. One day, Dad brought home some IHC volunteer badges to help fundraise for the charity. I thought it was a good idea to fundraise money, but instead of giving it to the IHC, I thought it would be more useful in my pocket. I stole the IHC charity badges and went collecting from the neighbours; people thought my sister and I were cute, but we were thieves in action. I felt bad doing this, but I also felt a sense of wild freedom, knowing I could do something like this and get away with it. Especially if there was an ice-cream at the end of it!

2

The Ingredients that Made the Cake

People must often wonder how a prostitute ends up being a prostitute. A cake needs certain ingredients to become a cake, and it's the same for the making of a prostitute.

My cake, however, didn't have the typical ingredients you would think; I had two parents, I went to Sunday School, and my father did not abuse me. The stereotypical upbringing of a prostitute often includes situations of an absent dad and childhood abuse.

I believe that our experiences in life shape who we are and how we see the world. For me, the traumatic experiences I had while being in hospital in those early years meant I was able to disconnect from reality by being an actress during times of hospital procedures. I was frequently changing schools, and my personality was being disrupted constantly. My fractured relationship with my mother left me fiercely independent, confused, and angry. I struggled to maintain friendships at school because I was always moving schools, and I was damaged from my early experiences in hospital.

When I was sixteen, I experienced my first abusive situation. I was celebrating New Year's Eve and got separated from my friends. I went along with a crowd of young people who were up to no good. I became isolated with a young man older than myself. He forced himself on me and I experienced a traumatic sexual assault. It took place in the bushes on a hill just by the celebrating city. I remember running away, falling down the tracks to get back to the city. I was shaking uncontrollably and my clothes were ripped. I clambered downhill and finally reached the roads that were filled with happy, celebrating people. I was in shock, cold inside and traumatised, yet joyful, excited people surrounded me. I found my way to the bus station and took the next bus home.

I was too scared to tell my parents at first, in case they banished me from the house forever. I believed I had got myself into that situation and that it was my fault. The next day, I eventually told my brother. My brother was going through some of his own hard stuff in life, and so my secret eventually came out to my parents.

Mum didn't handle the situation well and was angry at me for not telling them straight away, and for telling my brother, who was going through his own stuff. What didn't help was that I was told by my mother that the outfit I had worn that night had brought the unwanted attention. I think this hurt me more than the assault itself; I had never felt so ugly, so rejected and emotionally wounded.

Mum and Dad calmed down and took me to the police station and the hospital. This wasn't helpful at all. The police were so careless about the event; it was New Year's Eve. I had hardly a description or a name, and they suggested that even if he got caught and I went to court, it would just re-traumatise me. I went to the hospital and endured the invasive treatment process.

A feeling of hate filled me up so fast; hate towards myself, the world, and God. Alongside that was self-disgust and rage. I stopped sleeping unless I had the light on. The darkness just reminded me of the night it happened. I hated taking showers; I couldn't stand the sight of my body, and I started wearing big, baggy clothes. I hated myself and couldn't deal with the rage within.

One day, I grabbed my razor and just began slicing at my arms. Somehow cutting myself released the pain on the inside, the outside pain somehow making sense of it all, just for a moment.

I spent hours listening to rap, angry metal and anything that helped me make sense of the pain in my soul. I still believed in God, but I was angry at him; how could he allow such a thing? Was I in the devil's playground and by my free choice had I given way to him? Wasn't God bigger than the devil? I didn't look for answers because I'd already concluded in my mind that God had watched, allowed it, and left me alone.

This was an incredibly painful place to be as a teenager; feeling disrupted inside, abandoned by God, and rejected by my family. I was too hurt to think about the free will God gives man, and how we use that free will to do evil to one another. I didn't understand that suffering is a part of life. I blamed God, instead of experiencing him as the one who could heal me.

I didn't talk to anyone about this. All these questions tormented me inside. I wasn't the same person anymore, so I lost the connection with my friends. I didn't think they would understand. I lost the connection with my brother because I thought I had ruined his happiness by reaching out to him in the first place, and any church involvement I had was also fading because of my anger at God.

It was like suddenly I'd been sucked into a hole, and there was no one to talk to. I couldn't identify with Marie anymore, so anyone connected to me, like friends, family and my faith, quickly became disjointed people in my world.

Before I was raped, I had thoughts about leaving school, and this confirmed it. I felt like a totally different person now. How could I go back? I didn't even know who I was.

Waking up the day after it happened, I looked around my room. An icy feeling of terror grew inside of me. Everything was still in its place, everything was the same on the outside. It was me who was different. Something had changed in me. I felt like a completely different person inside now.

I left school immediately, unable to face my friends. I began working full time at a fast-food restaurant. Most of the people there smoked marijuana and took speed. I was so hungry for self-destruction and escaping reality that I easily slipped into that crowd of people. I identified with broken people trying to escape their pain and have some fun in a tragic world. Pretty soon, drugs became my best friend; they were always reliable and would faithfully take me away from reality. I was finally being able to access the freedom I yearned for as a child. I felt free inside for the moment when I was high, and no-one was going to control me or tell me what to do anymore.

My parents became increasingly aware that I was doing drugs. They took my sister to my grandparents' house, then sat me down. "Either you clean your life up and give up drugs or you move out!" I chose to leave. They believed that tough love was the best way to deal with a rebellious teenager.

THE INGREDIENTS THAT MADE THE CAKE

Mum and Dad had boxes for me to pack my things up, but I had no car, just my BMX bike and a room full of Eminem posters, music, clothes spilling out of the drawers and containers with pot hidden inside. Moving out was impossible, but so was staying home. I couldn't find the Marie I had always been. She was gone. Mum offered to quit her job and help me get clean, but I didn't choose this option.

I left home on my BMX bike with none of my things and nowhere to go. It became dark quickly, so I parked up outside an ANZ Bank ATM. It was in a sheltered area, so I curled up, hugging my knees to my chest, and slept there in the cold.

The next day, I went to a friend's house to call a new friend from the restaurant. He came over to pick me up and take me back to my home. I packed a few belongings, and he took me to his house.

My friend had his own room above his parents' garage. He offered I stay the night and sleep with him. This terrified me. After the assault, the idea of sex really turned me off. I hated people touching my body and the thought of someone seeing my self-harm scared me.

When I said no, he accused me of being frigid. I felt absolute shame standing there in his room, unable to sleep with him in exchange for a roof over my head.

3

Moving Day

I talked to my friends at the restaurant about what had happened. There were four workers that shared a large flat in the roughest neighbourhood in town. Eleven people lived there, including some children, and they immediately offered to take me in, as long as I was happy to share a room with children.

I went back and got the rest of my belongings that day and moved into a four-bedroom, two storied, rundown house with broken windows and unmown grass. Pot smoking was freely encouraged, and children scurried around like hungry cats. It was a far cry from my tidy, brick home in a new subdivision, but something in my broken spirit identified more with my new environment than my family's home.

The house was overrun with cockroaches, there were mattresses on the floor and double bunks in most bedrooms. Living there was another teenage runaway, a middle-aged gay man, my two managers from work, a husband of one of the ladies, and their five children, plus me.

My days and nights became focused around getting stoned or drunk, turning up to my shifts with clear-eye medicine just to make sure I wasn't fired. For the first year after the assault, I continued to stay away from guys. I was sexually timid and began dressing like a boy.

I spent days riding my BMX, growing dreadlocks and having facial piercings that told the world to fuck off. I had the freedom of being an adult now, but with the emotional wounds of a war victim. My personality was so disrupted that I found it very hard to process the emotions that were coming up. I hated my own body; it was a prison I couldn't escape. I resented my feminine frame and felt I was disgusting. I continued to cut my skin; physical pain would often release the emotion inside.

I woke up once, in the early hours of the morning, and the pain of reality flooded through me. I remember reaching for my bong and pulling open the windows, sitting up in my bunk and getting high, just to fall asleep again. It was then that I suddenly realised that I couldn't have the freedom of adulthood I saw as a kid. The sadness and pain inside was locking me up from ever being able to enjoy life again.

I thought about suicide a lot. If being an adult hurt this much, then why would I sign up for any more of life? Sadness became like an anchor in my soul, weighing me down in every area. I couldn't escape. Sometimes it would ease when I was stoned or cutting myself. I'd feel better temporarily, but I knew this world would pull me back to its harsh reality, either through nightmares in the night or having to work sober.

If I wasn't working or getting stoned in my bedroom, I would go to the local library and sit there for hours, stoned and sad, reading novels and journaling my inner pain. Living with ten people plus with their friends dropping in, I couldn't get much alone time and so the library became a place of safety. You can't talk out loud in there, so people would leave you alone. I would see young kids come in with their parents. It would fuel my bitterness towards life because I remembered coming to the library with my mum, this very library, as a kid. Now look at me, a few years later; stoned, sad, alone. Broken.

Some days, I would sit in the local graveyard near my house. When I wanted to talk to someone without them talking back, I would go there. I felt like I could really talk to people there. There was no judgement from dead people. They could listen and never say a word. They would take your secrets and you knew they were safe in the ground. There was something about the dead people that made me hope for a better life. Here I was alive, and they were dead, and yet I longed to swap places. Somehow, it spurred me on to try to live another day because I knew they would probably wish to be alive, especially the children buried there.

My parents and I seldom saw each other. My fighting with Mum escalated. Dad was trying to protect Mum from my arguing and also shelter my little sister, who still looked up to me and wanted me to play.

My sister and I were incredibly close, growing up, but this experience had rocked me inside and changed who I was, so that I felt I couldn't play with her anymore. Something grown-up had happened to me and I was now filled with hate and confusion. I stayed away from the family.

One day, I made a doctor's appointment for some medication. He referred me to see a therapist. I began to see a middle-aged man who had a caring face and always wore old shoes. He was from South Africa. He smiled a lot and seemed to be interested in trying to help me, but I found it too hard to review the assault or make sense of my childhood. I continued to get stoned and cut myself, despite attempts from him to help me. It was too raw and too painful, so instead I filled up the sessions talking about my current friendships or working life at the fast-food joint.

As my life spiralled out of control, I got into trouble more and more at the restaurant for drug and alcohol use. One day, my boss sent me home with a letter of termination. I immediately fell apart, spiralling into despair and shame. My flatmates shunned me a bit for getting fired; how come they were able to keep it in control and I wasn't? I was the weakest link in the group.

I signed up for an alternative education course, hoping it may lead to some kind of employment. During this course, I met an older man who showed some care and interest without asking too many questions. He gave me drugs to sell and if I sold enough, I would keep a bit for myself. We would hang out during the day while his wife was at work and his daughter was at school.

I was so reluctant to have any kind of sex with anyone, but the drugs he offered wore down my defences and I quickly found myself in a sexual relationship with him. I hated every second, yet I felt trapped. I had no income for buying drugs now and here he was offering me a lot in exchange for sex and if I sold some for him. It made me popular with my flatmates again too, because suddenly I had gone from being the weak link to the supplier.

Eventually I felt trapped. I knew sleeping with him was wrong and I wasn't attracted to him apart from the drugs. Every time he touched me, I felt sick. It quickly became too much to take. The drugs weren't worth it. Slowly I tried having this conversation with him, but he refused to listen, saying he was in love with me and he wanted to leave his wife. I was all of seventeen. He was nearly fifty.

I knew this wasn't good; I felt disgusting, used, and unable to say no. I was confused because I'd allowed it to happen. I didn't say no, and I appeared okay with it, but inside it just added to my shame and feelings of being owned.

One day I decided the answer to all my problems would be to kill him. I would kill him when he was unaware and then drive off with his car and all his drugs. Then I would get arrested and spend the rest of my life in a jail cell.

The thought of this gave me an exhilarating feeling of running to freedom; I thought this was a great idea! I wanted the world to just stop. The inner turmoil was like a cancer spreading deeper into my life. My flatmates only seemed to like me now because I was their source of drugs, but they still kept their distance because I was deeply disturbed; they knew I spent time in graveyards and they knew about the cutting. Even for drug addicts I was too much trouble. I concluded that the best option would be to go to jail; then perhaps everyone would leave me alone and I would have no problems.

Even my therapist was failing me. He was talking more with my parents, as the chaos of my life hit crisis point. I felt he was betraying any trust we had formed over the last year. I was also starting to feel owned by even my therapist, as he talking with my parents, and them making decisions about me was taking any control I had away from me.

Murdering this man would somehow solve all my problems. I felt trapped by him; I couldn't break it off, no matter how hard I tried. I needed the drugs, and if I went to jail I would have no more drugs, but maybe that's what I needed. I wouldn't have to pay rent in jail, and I wouldn't have my therapist. I would just settle for my life being one epic fail, and people would finally back off. I could spend the rest of my time alone, in a cell, and have no responsibilities.

I had a flatmate who was only fifteen years old. His dad had kicked him out of home and he spent most of his days getting stoned. I mentioned my plan to him and he agreed and offered to help. We would split the drugs and any cash he had. We plotted his murder carefully, but the night we went to carry it out, my friend bailed and left me alone in the house with this older man. I didn't want to raise any suspicion from him, so I asked him if he wanted a massage. I would do this by myself, and I didn't care if I got caught.

As it all unfolded, it became heart-wrenching and nerve-wracking. I had a plan, a weapon and determination. I sat on his back giving him a massage next to the fire; the heavy metal fire shovel by my hand. I kept relieving one hand away at a time, so he wouldn't get suspicious. I remember reaching for the fire shovel and pulling away, feeling sick. Suddenly, the reality of the situation dawned on me and I thought about his daughter. She would have no dad anymore. I couldn't imagine losing my dad. Despite the black, confusing world inside of me, clarity broke through the darkness and take a grip on my heart. I couldn't do it.

I felt sick at the sudden reality that if I killed him, I would have to answer to his family... and all that blood. I'd feel his skull crushing under my hand; my own little hand, innocent and clean. I was struggling to breathe now, just thinking of it. I excused myself early and went home, driving through the night sobbing. I wasn't sure if I was crying because of my hopeless situation or the fact I'd nearly murdered a man; a father, a husband. A human being.

4

The Doorway to a Whole New World

The next day I was sitting on the porch having a cigarette when my flatmate's boyfriend pulled up in his Mercedes. He was a plump, Greek-looking man, gay, dressed in a fancy white pressed shirt and well-groomed pants. He didn't belong in our neighbourhood, but he was dating my older flatmate. He walked up to me and asked if my flatmate was home. We didn't often chat because we had little in common. He owned a brothel in town and associated with people of a higher class than my own. It suddenly dawned on me that he could be my saviour.

"Hey... do you think I could work for you?" I asked.

He looked at me sitting on the steps with my cigarette in an oversized hoodie and matted, dyed blonde hair. "Hmm... how old are you?"

"Seventeen."

"You have to be eighteen, sorry."

"I'm eighteen in a month! I swear... please?" I smiled up at him, hoping he would take me under his wing. It was dawning on me that if I had money and independence, maybe I could be happy, and maybe I could be free from the problems I had.

He shrugged. "Come to the parlour tonight and we will sign you on. Do you have any clothes?"

"Not really..." I had been dressing like a tomboy since the assault a year and a half ago.

"We have some spare. See you tonight. You can start work now, but we will sign you in properly when you're 18. Keep that to yourself."

I was elated. I couldn't believe it! Sexually, I would be in control. I'd have money to pay the rent, I'd have money to buy drugs, and I'd have the ability to leave the married man I was trapped with. It was perfect!

From that day on I promised myself I'd never self-harm. This body would not be a victim anymore, but a body of power. People would want me and I'd be valued; valuable... I couldn't even fathom that someone would pay for me!

My first hour was upon me. I fitted into a tight pink tie-dyed dress. Tight was one word to explain it, as I had been eating plenty of the food at the restaurant I'd worked in. I wore borrowed black heels and tan pantyhose. I covered my self-harm marks with foundation and slipped on satin gloves up to my elbows. My hair was brushed and flowing down my back, and I held a little purse with my cigarettes and condoms.

The buzzer rang in the girls' lounge of the parlour. I could hear muffled voices.

My stomach was in knots. The other five ladies sitting around the girls' private lounge began putting out their cigarettes and gathering their heels.

"I bet it's fucking Singh and his gang. What time is it? Of course... they'd be finished work now. Here we go." An older lady who had years of sex work weathered deep into her pale, worn skin was slowly dragging on her heels and getting up.

"Ladies!" the house matron's voice called. I fell into line as we all began to file out into the guest lounge. I had no idea what to expect, but I was excited. Someone might just pay for me. I'd be in control!

I glimpsed myself in the mirror before filing out; I felt beautiful for the first time in a long time. I looked like a different girl, all dressed up. Something in me felt a strange sense of value that I hadn't felt before. I was about to get rich!

I walked into the lounge and saw three Indian men sitting side-by-side on the sofa. They looked us all up and down, one by one, with beady eyes. One muttered a hello but the other two just sat in silence. The other ladies warmly smiled but gave minimal encouragement. A sick sense of dread began welling up in my stomach.

"And this is Ashlee. She's new; brand-new today." The house matron gestured towards me and I felt them glue their eyes on me. The first man got up and walked over to the house matron and whispered in her ear. The house matron nodded and looked at me. "Room 5 Ashlee. 30 minutes."

It had begun. What if I didn't know what to do? Suddenly I freaked out. However, I remembered that as a child I could disconnect and find strength; don't cry, you're an actress, you're being paid not to cry. Then it clicked; I was Ashlee. I was an actress! And I was being paid, so shut up and don't cry.

I worked in that club for only a few months. I began to loathe the clients, who were 90% Indian. What bothered me was that they would come in groups of three. One at a time, they would book you while the others waited their turn.

Acting was becoming increasingly difficult and the money suddenly wasn't worth it; they usually only booked half an hour and the pressure for them to shower twice, have a massage and receive full service became too taxing. By the time I paid the house fee, my health pack and massage oils, I was left thinking, was it worth it?

I wasn't making any friends; most of the girls stuck to themselves and bitched about their childhood or the clients. I couldn't bitch much about my childhood; not compared to these girls. I knew my dad loved me; he never abused me, and my parents remained married. I knew my brother and sister adored me, too. I had a sexual assault experience, but that was still locked deep in my soul. It was hardly workplace banter. I also didn't have years of sex industry experience up my sleeve, so I was a bit of a fish out of water.

Sitting and listening to the girls talk about their lives, I couldn't help but feel sorry for them. I was brand new in this industry and hearing of their experiences; I knew I was in for a ride. For some reason, it didn't turn me away or scare me; life outside of a brothel was just as mean, in fact, it was worse. Here, I had some control, the comradery of other women, and money. It was just as shit as the real world, but here I got paid for it, and I could be somebody else.

The girls' lounge constantly had a cloud of cigarette smoke, and the pressure of working long hours was increasing. I heard about another club where the clients were screened more carefully. Only New Zealand men and wealthy foreigners were allowed, the bookings were an hour minimum, and the pay was better. I went over and began working at this club.

They gave me a much better experience than I had at the first club. They valued me more, the money was better, and the clients were much nicer. I wouldn't come out of a booking and have to see his friends as well; it was more of an elite clientele allowed in this brothel.

I began making friends here too. I was still smoking weed and snorting speed in my spare time, but my self-harm had completely stopped. I'd also lost the older, married boyfriend because he saw me in my working-girl clothes one day and thought I was disgusting. He didn't want to share me so he broke up with me completely. I felt freer than I had in years. It didn't last long, though.

After a long night at the brothel I would drop a girl home after work. She injected methadone daily, claiming it helped her sleep after work. I never feared needles after growing up around the hospital; in fact, they fascinated me. Watching the nurses do it, I'd often ask if I could learn to do it myself. I'd also watched 'Basketball Diaries' and 'Trainspotting' growing up. The life of a heroin addict was so tragic and wild, but it somehow appealed to my self-destructive nature. I identified my inner pain with the chaotic world of a junkie.

One day when I was dropping her off, she asked me if I wanted to come in and try some. I was instantly out of the car; I didn't even think twice. There was an excited sense of risk attached, and I knew I was destined for it.

The first time I injected, I felt a funny taste in the back of my throat. I could literally feel the fluid going through my vein and then an almighty overwhelming wave dropped over me as I collapsed onto the bed. I was hooked immediately. I had never experienced a deep bliss like this. It was the escape from my pain

I had been looking for. I was no longer in the real world. I was elsewhere... somewhere deep and pain-free. Unconscious.

I began injecting methadone with her after work and then on my days off. The feeling of slipping deep into unconsciousness became so addictive that this became a daily thing. It began interrupting my work as people would notice track marks. My bubbly personality also became hidden under the weight of addiction and the hangover effects of the drug.

5

The Wall

I was eighteen now. One day, my brother came to visit me and could see the addicted state I'd gotten myself into. I was half passed out in my bunk and saw him enter the room. I knew then I couldn't lie to him, I couldn't hide that my life was a wreck. He stayed about ten minutes, but then he went home and he joined forces with my parents to bring me back home to get clean.

My brother came back that evening and told me I had to come with him. I knew what was happening, but I didn't fight it. He and my parents had sat down and decided I had to get help. Days earlier I'd crashed my car through a fence with my young flatmate, the same one who had helped me to plan the murder.

Things had gotten really bad at my flat; they'd become aware that I was disturbed and they were starting to talk about kicking me out.

It all happened in such a short time, but within a couple of months of using methadone, I had lost nearly everything. I found it hard to keep appearances up at the elite brothel, my flatmates were even more distant from me and I was now physically addicted and had lost all self-control.

I agreed with my parents that rehab was the answer. They found a rehab in the country and called to make arrangements for the next day.

That night I slept on my sister's bedroom floor, tossing and turning and feeling violently ill. A migraine drove me to vomit in the middle of the night. Even though I knew I needed drugs, the fight in me was completely gone and I stayed through until morning to go to rehab. I had nothing left to lose.

Rehab was a different experience from hospital. I shared a room with a sweet young girl who was on a police bail watch. There were people just like me, strung out, faces without hope, and nearly everyone was rail thin.

The withdrawals were horrible. I had intense headaches and vomiting, and when I did sleep I had lucid nightmares. I dreamed that I had woken up and murdered everyone in the rehab. When I woke up in the morning I was too scared to get out of bed to see if I actually had murdered everyone during the night; it was that real to me!

The pain in my arms was like someone pulling at my veins. I desperately needed methadone. I felt like I was dying.

During that time, I once again prayed to God. I also prayed to the devil. I either needed methadone or I needed freedom. I cried out and said, "Satan, you need to get me out of here. I'll use drugs. I need them. Please help me! But God, if you want to step in, then fine. I can't handle this anymore!"

I remember crying myself to sleep. During the night, this deep physical churning in my guts woke me. I remember trying to wake up from this sleep state, but somehow I knew to let it happen; it was God!

Something inside of me knew it was the hand of God. It was breaking something loose from within me; the big, fat snake of addiction that had owned me was breaking and leaving my body. It was a surreal experience. When it stopped I lay there, feeling like something was missing... the addiction! It was gone! I'd literally cried out to God in the night and asked him to help me, to take it away.

I was very aware of the reality of God and Satan. I'd learned a lot in Sunday school as a kid and from things my parents had taught me over the years; about God's ability to heal and answer prayers and set you free from pain. I'd heard that over the years, but now I *knew* that side of God. I met the compassion and mercy of God, listening to me and actually helping me; a prostitute and a drug addict! It reminded me that, as a child, I had loved God and felt he loved me.

I got out of bed the next morning and felt freer than I had been in years.

That same morning, my roommate woke up terrified. She said she'd seen evil spirits lurking in our room and then leaving suddenly. I knew what had happened, but wondered if she'd believe me. I told her I had prayed to God and felt something evil leave me from inside. She stared at me wide-eyed, but couldn't deny what she had seen.

I knew I had a long way to go, though. I'd made such a mess of it all, but now I knew I could ask God for help and he would help me.

I still had the memories of drugs and sex and money, and when rehab was hard, I'd think back at those times and long to go back. One thing that began triggering it all again was whenever I had conversations with other residents about drugs. It was like I'd forget that God helped me, and I'd only think about drugs again.

I began sneaking out at night to go back to my flat and get stoned, returning in the morning before everyone woke up. I only did this a couple of times, because the hitchhike rides took a long time coming.

Rehab didn't last too long. It was meant to be for 12 months but after only a couple of months I got into an argument with another girl and left. This was my opportunity to go straight back to drugs if I wanted, but that day God came back into my consciousness strongly; he wanted to help me. I had a tiny bit of hope, so I hitch-hiked back to my parents' house. To my surprise, they welcomed me in and I began to live life again from home.

I started going to church and tried really hard to clean up my life. I no longer snuck out to get weed or alcohol. In fact, I even started reading my Bible.

One day, I was called into the doctor's office. The nurse sat me down and unfolded to me my latest test results. "I'm sorry, Marie. You have Hepatitis C," she explained.

Really? I thought back to how I'd shared needles and hadn't even cared.

Suddenly, receiving that diagnosis, I felt sick to my stomach. I'd walked to the doctor's, thinking nothing much of the invite there, so now, heavy with this new diagnosis, I had to walk home to my family and tell them the news. That walk home was the longest walk of my life. I was overwhelmed by the fact that I might die. There was a sense of shame and disgust. I had brought this one upon myself.

Telling my brother was the hardest of all. He had put a lot of effort into helping me get clean again. We didn't get along very well most of the time, but we had a deep bond underneath it all.

Mum went on red alert for germs and brought disinfectant and gloves. She banished me from cooking in the kitchen, paranoid that I was infectious. I look back now and smile a bit, but it hurt at the time; I already felt such shame and disgust. Mum was acting, not reacting. She was trying to protect the rest of the family. We were both still coming to terms with the fact we lived together again after years of arguments.

I felt isolated and began talking to God more through this time. When I had the energy, I would go for walks and chat with him. I even began going to a youth group for a while. I found it hard fitting in there, because of the life I'd just come out of. Compared to the perfect-appearing goody two-shoe kids, I was out of place, often over-sharing my story and what I felt God had led me out of. I don't remember forming any close friendships through this time.

I knew God was real, and he had helped me in my life, but this felt like a unique relationship compared to how the other kids prayed to him. They didn't swear or smoke, or even question God. My Bible readings in the morning often included a cigarette out in the morning sun, and my prayers were laced with colourful language.

The next couple of months after that were a real blessing. I rested, slept, ate, read my Bible and continued to go on walks. Mum was healing towards me; she was accepting of my rough-around-the-edges state and my new relationship with God. Mum understood what it was like to be real and gutsy in her relationship with God; she never sugar-coated anything. I could see this was a good side of her; the result of her being broken by life's difficult circumstances.

If I was ever tempted to use drugs again, I now had the diagnosis of Hepatitis C looming over me, reminding me of the high price that using needles had cost me.

My diagnosis disturbed my brother. He first offered me his own liver so that I could live. I remember being in his bedroom and he was upset with the possibility of losing me. He turned and asked if he could give me his liver, but I knew it was impossible; he might die. After this, he began to disconnect and appeared very angry towards me. I was unsure why, but Mum suggested it was his way of coping.

One day I was in my bedroom and I felt God speak a thought into my mind, "Do you want to be healed?" I checked the thought and decided it must be God. It wasn't my own, was it?

"Of course I do. That's a stupid question!" I kind of shrugged it off and didn't think much about it.

Two weeks later, I was called back to the specialist's office. I was getting ready to go on a trial drug that would help me stay alive. "Your test results have just come back... and this is highly unusual... in fact... very rarely has this ever happened that I have seen... but the hepatitis C has left your body." He looked at me and I looked back at him, stunned.

"Really? How?" I asked.

"Your tests show it came in your body and has left again. You now have antibodies. You can't catch it again and you're not infectious," he said.

I looked over at Mum. "I think God healed me," I said.

Mum was beaming. She was so shocked and full of excitement, as was the doctor.

I went home after that, totally free. I left the shame and disgust on the floor of the doctor's office that day. And I knew God was real!

6

Rebuilding

Despite this encounter with a miracle, I began to struggle again. As the next few months rolled by, I started smoking weed again and drinking heavily. I went to my friends place one day to tell them about God, but they laughed at me and told me I needed some weed, and in that home, in that environment, my old identity came flooding back and I caved in and got stoned. I never mentioned God to them again.

God must have done something strong in me though during the few months I'd isolated at home, because I never went back to using methadone. But I couldn't understand why I was still dabbling in things of my past. Why hadn't I been stronger?

I began an outpatient rehab in New Zealand but eventually booked into a rehab in Australia for a year and a half. It was an all girl's home, only 12 girls in all of Australasia were accepted. I didn't think I was a bad case, but there was something wounded in me still, that kept me locked in addiction, despite my miracle. I had deep unresolved issues that needed healing, and I knew the girl's home in Australia could help me resolve these.

There was a waiting list for nine months and during this time I did a boot-camp for six months. This worsened my drinking and pot smoking, though. Despite the gruelling training, I still got myself wasted every night. I'd pray to God for forgiveness the next day, and cry as it happened all over again.

After the nine-months wait, I was accepted and flown to Sydney. I stayed in the programme for a year and a half. I became best friends with a girl named Jaye. She and I came in around the same time and graduated the same time. We had a year and half full of memories; living together in close quarters, and bonding through the difficulties of living with 12 troubled girls.

When we graduated, the staff gave Jaye and me a red Toyota Corolla to share. We named it Sally. Life was good then. I continued to live in Australia for a while and worked in a coffee shop. I got my barista certificate and trained up to be a team leader in the shop.

On the weekends I went to Hillsong Church, and I lived in a flat of Christian girls. These girls were fun, and we got along really well. I had worked on most of my unresolved issues and was using the tools I'd learned to manage my daily life outside of rehab. Jaye and I were both doing well since graduating; not one relapse.

We decided it would be good if we did something meaningful with our lives. I signed up for a counselling degree back in New Zealand and she decided to stay on in Australia and do her social work degree. Jaye kept Sally and went home to live in Maitland with her parents, to study. I flew home to New Zealand and embarked on a counselling degree.

Six months later I was sitting in the library one day, finishing an assignment, a day before the holidays started, when I got a phone call from Brittany, a girl who had also been very close to Jaye and I in the girls' home.

"Jaye's dead! She's committed suicide," the girl said.

I couldn't comprehend that. What? I broke down immediately and left for home. I drove home sobbing in shock, desperate to call her mum to confirm this How could this be? She and I were meant to be doing something meaningful with our lives. We even made a pact to stay on track and move forward in life.

Sadly, I got home and couldn't get hold of her mum. I got hold of Renee, a staff member of the girls' home, who had remained a close support since our graduation. She confirmed that Jaye had committed suicide the day before.

I was so angry. For some reason, I wanted to refuse to go to the funeral. I couldn't understand how she would do something like that! Another staff member of the girls' home said I had to go to the funeral; I'd regret it if I didn't, and she booked me a flight immediately.

I flew over to Australia for the funeral, but I hadn't wanted to go. It was the saddest and most heart-wrenching funeral I have ever experienced. I was cold with shock, surrounded by people sobbing, watching the white coffin up the front and hearing her family say she had finally done something for herself, as she was always helping others.

I couldn't contain my emotions. Usually I'd be disconnected, somehow numb in situations like this, like the actress, being paid not to cry. This was too much. I broke down and sobbed and sobbed.

It took the wind out of my sails. I thought a lot about what she must have gone through. Why didn't she call? How come she did such a sad thing to herself? I knew I'd felt suicidal in the past, but watching her family carry her coffin out of the church playing her favourite song, I vowed I would never do that to my family.

I went back to New Zealand and continued my university degree. I had to get help from the learning center, but my grades began to go from C's, to B's to A's. In my final year, I was cracking out A+ essays and getting high scores on my practicums.

Mum and Dad were really supportive of me during this time; Mum baked me a pudding every time I got an A. She was a strong support during these years, meeting me for lunch every week to hear how I was going.

The years going by had healed Mum a bit, and she and I developed a strong bond for the first time. I loved my studies, and I was in a great girls flat with my sister.

I enjoyed counselling so much. I loved making sense of why people were the way they were. I enjoyed listening; nothing shocked me, and I was led by compassion and empathy, but learnt the skills to help others figure themselves out. It was a real rush to have a client come in with what seemed like a big mess, and then leave with a clearer sense of the picture, with tools to help them get on with life. It was great. I felt like my purpose in life was becoming completed.

On the outside, life was going really well. I was in a great flat, I was soaring through my degree and I was keeping fit and healthy. I still felt pain and anger about losing Jaye; some days I would over-exercise and run for ages, sometimes twice a day. I would restrict my food to lose weight, to get ultimate results, and somehow feel like I was in control of everything. I kept that part of me secret, never discussing it in my counselling class.

Many people mentioned my weight loss. I wasn't sure if this fuelled my disorder or hindered it. I would feel validated inside that I had lost weight but also a sense of shame that it was because I had unresolved issues. Something plagued me that the girls' home hadn't fixed; something that studying counselling hadn't fixed. I would often brush off their comments and change the subject.

I stopped getting my periods and began having to get heart check-ups. My addictive personality was being fed, and I thrived on restricting food and overdoing exercise. Despite my life finally going smoothly, the self-destruction demon continued to play havoc in my life.

7

A Storm is Brewing

I worked for a couple of years in the counselling field before getting restless. I was now around 25 and I wanted to travel. One day I applied to be a youth security officer on a cruise ship. Within a week I was interviewed and hired!

It all started with such a big, exciting bang. They flew me over to Australia to do training for a couple of days, before embarking on my first cruise liner. I was inducted on the ship and then released to work my 11 hour shifts, 7 days a week with a co-worker, with whom I shared a cabin. The first few weeks were a dream: we worked, then we partied, then we slept, worked and partied.

During this time, I experienced a sexual encounter with a workmate who wouldn't take no for an answer. I was in the crew bar drinking when an Indian man began hitting on me. I was not attracted to him and fobbed him off Thinking he was gone, I continued to party, and then went to my cabin in the early hours of the morning. I could see the man following me but I thought it was a bit of a joke and told him to go home to his bed. He continued to follow me and when we got to my cabin, he peeled the key off me and forced me into my cabin. My cabin-mate was working and suddenly this was no joke anymore. I tried to force him off but my efforts were in vain. He silenced me with his hand and his sexual desires took over.

This triggered all of my old wounds reopening, and I felt like this was my lot in life. I remember him rushing off afterwards, and I was left angry and shocked.

I lay there in unbelief. Again? Seriously? I felt that wave of disappointment roll over me; the same wave that I had experienced many times before. Life had been going well, and then wham... a huge, shocking issue again. I became that angry teenager who was lost and hurt all over again.

I told the security boss the next day and got tests by the on-board doctor. Video footage outside my cabin showed the man forcing himself into my room, and he was kicked off the boat. They gave me the option to leave, but I stayed on.

I just began to party even harder. I began mixing some painkillers they gave me for a tooth extraction with alcohol, partly to help me sleep and partly just to get wasted.

I left the boat after my partying caused me to collapse one day while I was working. The captain was angry at how much I had partied and said he wanted me to leave the boat and get help.

I returned to New Zealand and stayed with my brother and his wife for six weeks. During this time, I dialled down my partying to almost nothing.

I enjoyed spending time with his wife, who was on maternity leave with her second child. For the first time in my family, I felt not judged, just accepted, and things were made light of. We'd watch TV during the day, do housework, cook tea and talk about life, and then, when my brother came home from work, we would chill some more.

This was really healing for me. I began to pick myself up again, and then, when I got enough strength, I bought a ticket to Thailand. I thought that maybe it would give me time to relax, maybe time to think about my next step. My sister-in-law was incredibly helpful during this time and was supportive of me getting my bearings for the world again; a trip to Thailand may be just what I needed.

I holidayed in Thailand for a couple of months before returning to New Zealand. Then I felt lost. I'd had my big holiday, I'd stayed long enough at my brother's and I was now ready for more work.

I couldn't go back to counselling because I was an emotional mess. I was avoiding the shameful glances and comments from people; extended family, classmates, anyone who had known of me during my counselling years. What was I doing now? How come I wasn't as vibrant, fit and healthy, emotionally or physically, as I had looked during those years? I really thrived during those counselling years, and here I was, trying to not die emotionally in the gutter of life.

After Thailand, I used my last bit of money to rent a caravan at the beach. I was trying to live a healthy, relaxed lifestyle, but still had this unresolved pain of abuse.

The first weekend that I was home, I went to a party with an old school friend. There was a rough-looking fisherman there that night. Everyone was drinking outside, but he was in the kitchen with a select few, handing around a meth pipe. I had no fears about new drugs. In fact, like old times, it excited me. I joined the group and told them it was my first time. They helped me by showing me how to smoke it. Immediately, I was hooked. I felt high, fast, alert, totally confident, and suddenly, very attracted to the fisherman.

He was a scruffy and rough bloke, but he didn't care. He didn't care about society and wanted to get high for the rest of his life. I could relate to him because I also hated society, and I also wanted to get high all my life. I could be myself around him, with no pretences and no expectations.

I was living near the beach in a caravan, living off my savings and unsure of my next step. Mum and Dad were still in my life, but our catch-ups were strained because of my emotional caginess and shame around the change that had happened in me. My sister was flatting with mutual friends and I remember it being hard to see her and appear to be okay. I knew she looked up to me and I hated knowing I was just a shadow of my former self.

I met a guy called Shane at a party. He was about my age and we got along really well together. We shared similar views on life. Soon after meeting him, I invited him to stay with me in my caravan and we got high on meth for about two weeks straight.

One day, Shane said that the meth was running out and he would have to stop. I couldn't imagine my life without meth now; it gave me so much purpose. I knew instantly how to solve the problem. I looked at him and confidently said I could pay for it. Meth had become like a baby to us. It had connected us together, but now was also our central focus.

I had been a sex worker before; now that I was older, I felt I was wiser and could do it properly this time. I felt that last time I had been naïve and didn't know my rights, therefore I was subject to the owners of the brothel telling me who and when and what to wear. I was smarter, I'd be in more control and this time I'd have meth as my friend through it all. Meth made me feel like I could do anything.

8

An Old Foot in a New Shoe

My new boyfriend Shane and I moved out of the caravan to his dad's property in the country. We had a huge shed in the backyard, like a big metal barn, two stories high. Shane and I had mattresses on the ground and a large wooden table by the window, on the second storey. We thought we were in heaven!

We would sit at the window smoking meth all day and all night, talking about society, the world, sharing drug stories and occasionally sleeping together on the mattress. His friends would sometimes drop by and we would all hang out and talk about anything, everything and nothing till all hours of the night.

I began going to work. It was weird for both of us at first. I reassured him it wasn't cheating because it was not love, it was a physical act using protection, under a different name and dressing up like a rock star. I told him not to worry and that I would be safe. He took a while to convince, but he also was pulled in by the love of meth. He compromised his values and allowed me to go off to work.

I loved the new club immediately. The girls were friendly and most of them looked clean from drugs and could hold a normal, friendly conversation. I had brought my own clothing this time and purchased a pair of red heels that would become my trademark.

My first job was an outcall. I was told that a very wealthy man, a famous musician known to the club by his frequent order of girls, was requesting to see the newbie. I was excited. I could get along with anyone and I knew it would be great money and probably a really good time. I packed my little purse and got into the house-matrons' car.

"Now Roxy... You can't talk too much; he doesn't like chatter. And you may as well leave your purse behind," she instructed.

"But what about the condoms?" I asked.

She shot me a sideward glance. "He doesn't like them very much, but it's up to you... if you want to stay and last with him then I would put up with what he wants."

"But isn't that illegal?" I asked. I was recalling the strict instructions given to me just hours before, to kick a man out if he refuses protection.

"You're on an outcall... you're not in the club. It's at your own discretion."

We pulled up at a set of iron gates with two security guards standing outside, hands clasped in front.

The lady gestured for me to get out. "He will call me when he's finished. Good luck. Not many girls stay too long."

She gave me a wink and watched me get out of the car. She made it sound like a potential house of horrors! My stomach began to churn. He's rich and famous, so how bad could it be?

They let me through the gates and I walked to the front door.

"Ma'am I need your purse." The guard motioned for my purse before opening the door. "He won't let any recording devices in the house. You need to hand in your purse," he said.

I was reluctant. "What about my cigarettes?" I asked.

"You will be given some up there."

"Oh." I handed over my purse and suddenly realised that without my phone or protection I was alone and vulnerable. He opened the door and I stepped into the foyer.

In front of me was a tall, wooden staircase and right at the top was the client, staggering his way down the stairs. He was muttering and mumbling to me. I tried to introduce myself, but he waved his hand at me. "I don't care," I managed to make out.

He looked me up and down and then continued to stagger around. I followed him like a little lamb, being quiet and attentive; wondering what he wanted. He led me back upstairs to panoramic views. His appliances, couches and TV were all so fancy and new, yet the house was a complete mess. Ashtrays and empty bottles lay everywhere.

He handed me a packet of cigarettes. "Can you cook?"

I nodded "Sure..."

"I want a beef stir-fry thing." He stumbled to the kitchen.

"Sure." I began to look for things, trying to find pots, pans, even the beef, but he suddenly changed and turned at me.

"What are you doing in my kitchen? No... that's not going to work."

He motioned me down a hallway, passing several bedrooms. I noticed another girl in one as I went past. He opened the door to the end room. A big, white king-sized bed sat in the middle of the room. An older woman was sprawled out on top. She smiled up at him.

"Wait here until I want you." He pushed me inside and closed the door.

I shivered inside. "This is so weird," I whispered to the woman lying on the bed.

She moved over and patted the mattress. "Here..." she gestured.

"What's going on?" I climbed onto the bed and lay next to her.

She shrugged. "Oh he's that way all the time. First time here?" she asked. I nodded. She laughed and pulled herself up to a sitting position. I noticed the TV on the wall was playing porn. She caught my eye looking at it "That stays on. We can't change the channel. Seriously, get used to waiting."

Wow... the weirdest first job ever!

I spent most of the time talking with my new friend; she was a private girl who worked for herself. She had plenty of experience at the house. I couldn't understand how he didn't want to use protection. I was determined to not play by his rules.

Time dragged on until I almost couldn't wait to leave. I needed to get high and I knew I had to contact my boyfriend. Shane was often paranoid about my whereabouts, partly for safety and partly because he wanted to make sure I was working and not with another man.

Finally, the man reappeared. He began seeing if I was sexually interested, but stopped when I said that unless he had protection it wasn't going to happen. This made him angry, and he left the room and returned with a paper bag. "Put this over your head! You're leaving!"

He began dialling numbers on his phone and I reluctantly put the paper bag over my head, my heart pounding. I could vaguely make out his muttering on the phone, but I knew he was calling my driver. Then I felt him march me out, down the hall and attempt to get me down the stairs. I began arguing about the paper bag, but he refused to let me take it off.

Before I knew it, I was outside. He ripped it off and handed me to the guards.

Rain had begun falling and I was put outside the gates with my purse. Thank God it was over!

The guards didn't speak, they just stood there next to me waiting for the driver. I was furious at his rudeness and paranoia, but so grateful to be out. The man re-appeared and handed me an envelope. "Don't come back," he spluttered.

Fury turned to relief... I'd got money. How much? I waited for him to leave before I took a peek inside. It looked enough, but man, it was almost not worth it.

There were two high-profile clients that were regulars at that brothel. Both were the meanest, nastiest clients and he was one of them. I didn't have to have sex with either of those men. Instead, they played a game of power and control.

One man would sail down from Auckland on his boat. He'd invite you to dinner, he would drink excessively, talk to you about how rich he was and how messed up you were to be a prostitute. He would say he could make your life better if you became his girlfriend, although then he could stop paying for you... were you worth paying for? What happened to you as a child that made you a sex worker? He would spend hours berating you. He would pay full price, pour expensive wine down your throat and feed you steak and chocolates.

The job sounded incredibly enticing, but stuck in his presence was soul-destroying. For some sick reason he liked me. He would hire me every Friday night for hours at a time. I was told I would lose my job if I didn't agree to go. Despite being contracted to the brothel, I still was told what to do and who to see.

One weekend, he became too much to bear. I picked up my coat and left him midway through the dinner. I called the driver and got her to collect me, and cried all the way back to the club.

My manager was furious that I had let down a high-profile client, but the mental abuse was torture. All the girls agreed and supported me to not go back. He was running out of options, as most girls were aware of his emotional abuse.

Most of the other clients that came through became regulars. They were middle-class men, some who would save up and have a fun time for an hour or so. The regular ones would treat you nicely and build a friendship with you throughout the process. I loved this side because I connected well with them, making each one feel special and unique. I functioned well in these 'friendships'. They were without commitment; I never felt trapped or owned because they would come for an hour and leave again until the following week.

I could maintain relationships easier without the commitment. The conversations were always superficial and pleasure orientated. For an hour, I could appear perfect, bubbly and innocent. I could pull it off, like the actress I knew I could be. I thrived in the fantasy world of 'Roxy,' dressing up like somebody else, pleasing people, being loved for an hour then let go to be myself again.

I still smoked meth at work, even though it was taboo. Most of the girls I worked with in this club were not drug users. That surprised me and, for some reason, I liked that. It was less drama. I kept the meth to myself, using it in the room after a booking, while I was cleaning the room, or I would hide away in the bathroom.

I got on well with one girl, Jo. She was a single woman in her early forties. She had rock-star blonde hair and a beautiful figure. She had a teenage daughter who was often up to mischief at school, but she seemed like a nice kid. Jo still had a sense of innocence about her and saw her work as being important. She would tell people she was in healthcare and a support worker; she felt she was taking care of their health and supporting the men; just in a sexual way.

There was a sense of pride in the club too. Girls were encouraged to be classy and modest, not so revealing, and to be professional always. I worked there for about a year.

9

A Tumultuous Relationship

It was becoming difficult for my boyfriend, Shane. Even though I liked the job and I saw it as work rather than cheating, I knew he didn't share the same belief. He stayed at home smoking meth, which made him increasingly paranoid. We began fighting continuously at home. I would arrive home and he would be pacing the floor, waiting for me. He would throw his accusations towards me with venom and built-up hatred. I tried convincing him I was working, but he believed I was elsewhere.

He began timing my trip home, calling me at work and sending threats through text messages. He became so angry and paranoid that I was cheating that he threatened to send his gang friends to work to teach me a lesson; I would have no idea when or who, as he said he would organise for me to have a private booking and it would be sprung on me.

A TUMULTUOUS RELATIONSHIP

I began to think it was my fault. I constantly tried to calm him down and make him see that work was work and home was home, and there was no other man romantically involved in my life. Even though I liked my clients, I was never romantically attracted to them. I did my best to not talk about work at home in case I fuelled his jealousy. I even offered to quit my job, but we both knew we needed money for our meth baby to be kept alive. I was growing attached to my workmates now, and the regular clients.

Shane became paranoid that his father or someone was poisoning him and bugging us. He started searching the house for listening devices, and often refused to talk in case people were listening. He became violent too when we argued, threatening to hurt me or kill me. I was madly in love with him and thought I had somehow aggravated him, and that it was my fault.

I was desperate to help him so one night we drove away with no plan, we would find a motel on the road, because pre-booking was not an option for paranoid Shane. Despite choosing one from the roadside he believed people had gotten there before us and bugged the room. He searched light bulbs, behind furniture and under the rugs for bugs. He refused to calm down and turned his aggression towards me. I fled. I ran off into the streets in the middle of the night and began hitchhiking away. I had a friend from my childhood, Ben, who lived near the beach; I could stay there.

Shane came over a couple of days later, begging my forgiveness. I missed our good times and so I agreed to go back. This didn't last long. One night he snapped again, but this time towards his dad, who called the police. He was arrested and taken away. I felt this was my opportunity to leave him and break free. I moved into Ben's flat and stayed plugged into work.

It was difficult breaking up with Shane because suddenly my loneliness highlighted the false love my work really was. I would now go home at night or in the early hours of the morning to sleep alone in a single bed. I had my meth and that was when my addiction grew. I began realising that my clients would come and see me for an hour, we would pretend to be lovers for that time and then break away for another week. However, they had families to go home to; they had lives and jobs and people. I would leave work and have my meth or sometimes my flatmates, but even then I felt disconnected from people, because my flatmates had normal lives. I felt lonely.

Around that time, I began seeing a man privately. I met him through a friend, and we would use drugs and sleep together. I never intended to leave work, but one day it all came crashing down.

There was a heavy man that came through to see me one day. Often, men would come in and act disrespectfully. He was not outwardly abusive, but was quite rude and aloof. After he had finished, he let out a huge sigh and dropped his body weight down on top of my small, thin frame. I felt a twinge at first and got out from underneath. I felt a bit of pressure near my ribs, but nothing major. I continued the shift without too much worry. I complained he was heavy and a bit rude and disrespectful to just collapse on me like that.

However, the next morning I woke up struggling to breathe. It hurt so much near my ribs that it was impossible to go to work. I could hardly get out of bed. I went into work and told my boss about the heavy man the day before and how I was finding it really hard to breathe. "It's probably just bruising. We really need you today; we're short staffed," the house matron said. She patted me on the back and turned away to keep doing her paperwork. I knew she was right; we were short staffed. It was the nature of this club;

the girls were lovely and the clients much better, but if you had been hurt you were expected to keep going.

I always soldiered on. I was a people pleaser, and I wanted to be loved and accepted by my boss and be a part of the club family. I hadn't seen my actual family now for over a year. I was missing my boyfriend and I knew that the club was the closest thing to a family I'd had in a while.

I tried to continue working that day with the sore ribs. I saw a few clients, but remember struggling to make the bed or clean the shower after every job. I made an appointment to see a doctor.

The next day I saw my family doctor. I hadn't seen a doctor in years, partly because of my meth use. I was afraid they would call the police or catch on and contact my family. Bravely I confessed to working in the club and explained what had happened. I was sent for an x-ray and it confirmed I had fractured two ribs on the right side. They couldn't strap it or anything; there was nothing they could do.

I was told I had to have six weeks off work. Six weeks! I needed the money, plus I had nothing else in my life that was keeping me busy. I had no hobbies or friends outside of the brothel, except my two flatmates who worked full time. I did not see this as an option.

I went back to my boss and told her the news. She was furious. I asked if I could do office work but she shook her head. I had been with them for a year now, arriving for every shift, being positive, a good worker and soldiering on through tough times. I had made friends and had regular clients, and probably made them more money than I'd made myself, yet I was let go on the spot.

"I'm sorry Roxy but if you can't work you need to be replaced." She said it with no compassion in her voice. I was devastated. So much for family!

I went home and contacted my doctor. Surely, he had to make this better? Were there any medications I could use? He suggested going on ACC; paid accident compensation. Besides, I had been working in a brothel which was a legal business, therefore I would be entitled to ACC. Awesome!

Brothels are legal in New Zealand. Girls are contracted to work through them, not as employees but as contractors. But if you are contracted the brothel is excused from having to pay any ACC or sick pay for you. However, most brothels operated with the characteristics of owning you as an employee. You were told what hours to work, what to wear, who to see, and how much to charge.

I contacted ACC before I knew that I was contracted. I didn't know if I was employed or contracted. The ACC case manager asked me lots of questions. Was I told what time to turn up and when to leave? Yes. Was I told who to see? Yes. Was I told what to wear? Yes. Was I told how much to charge? Yes. Then I was employed, therefore I was entitled to ACC. Awesome. This would keep me alive during time off work.

However, it turned out that the brothel had contracted me; I had signed a contract. I was a contract sex worker according to the club. How come I had been treated like an employee for a year? If they had been operating the girls as employees, with no rights to their own work independence, then they were practicing unfairly and illegally. The brothel gets out of paying ACC and sick-pay yet are reaping the benefits of having girls thinking they are employed, submitting to club rules and charges, but not aware of their independence as contractors.

I had discovered the flaw in the system. Yes, it was legalised, but it was running illegally. Girls did not know their rights! This became very dangerous ground for me; I knew if I blew the lid on this, my life was at stake.

I learnt that, depending on if I was an employee or contractor, my rights and responsibilities would differ. The brothel stated I was an independent contractor, therefore they had no responsibility toward my ACC. However, according to the practice within the brothel, all girls were treated as employees.

A TUMULTUOUS RELATIONSHIP

I was faced with a decision whether to take them to court; not just to win ACC because they treated me as an employee, but to make a statement to other New Zealand girls in brothels. They must know their rights and be treated accordingly, not be owned or subjected to the employment regulations as independent contractors. This became very exciting and scary. I was advised by several lawyers that this would be a very dangerous case, but I should pursue it.

At that time, there was another high-profile case in the media where a sex worker took the brothel to court and, in the first case in New Zealand history, she was awarded compensation and the brothel was reprimanded. Should I do the same?

One night, a girl from our brothel stole some money she felt she was owed by the high-profile, famous client. She was busted before she even left his house and was beaten up severely by his bodyguards, and not being able to present herself back to work that night looking spotless and beautiful, she was fired. No one said a word about the violent consequence she endured.

Unfortunately, her family had gang connections. The gang appeared at his house and threatened to take over. He called the police and when the police arrived, they found his house full of sex workers and drugs. The media had a huge hay-day with this and began interviewing some of the sex workers who worked there. We were all bound by confidentiality, but it was also drummed into us the danger of speaking out in public and bringing shame upon the brothel. It was hinted that you would be endangering yourself if you spoke out, and that the brothel had protection from local gangs.

This situation was huge at the time. The media journalists would come in, pretending to be clients, to get information on our high-profile client. Some girls talked outside of the brothel to journalists and told of the unprotected sex, drug use and exploitation that was frequently operating. I was lucky enough to be called to his house only twice; he got the message I wasn't going to have unprotected sex and I was never asked back. I was hugely relieved.

I never spoke to the media because when I was there, I never saw any drugs and I knew causing trouble by breeching confidentiality would mean the loss of my job. The fear of unknown and unspoken consequences also loomed around me like a silent threat.

This situation was my indicator not to pursue the court case against the brothel. I was too cautious of the 'what ifs'. The brothel was like a family, but despite it being legal and in the public eye, a lot of the unspoken rules and regulations to be part of that family ran underground, that only you would see or know but never talk about if you were a working girl.

10

A Fast Exit onto a New Level

Shortly before I lost my job because of my broken ribs, I had begun frequently seeing an older man on the side. He would pay me in drugs, copious amounts, but we would have fun together and often go on trips for days at a time. He was like a big kid inside, yet I knew he was also a big timer in the meth world.

He wouldn't say much about his meth world, but he didn't have to. He didn't work, he owned several fast cars and motorbikes, carried kilos of meth and a suitcase full of other drugs. He dealt only in cash and he never talked much about what he got up to. I put two and two together but was smart enough to just enjoy his company and not ask questions.

Very quickly we became a couple, although he lived several hours away. We had a relationship built on drugs and frequent trips to see each other. He would pick me up and take me to hotels for a few days, or I would go and live with him for a while. I felt I had hit the jackpot. He was fun, dangerous and generous. I didn't have to go back to work and I had access to endless amounts of meth.

I look back now and can see it was the meth that glued us together. I couldn't be with a boyfriend who didn't share the habit because, well, what would we talk about? I smoked the pipe most of the day, who would I share this with? However, in the beginning I genuinely liked him.

When he was away I would send him photos of myself, to make him miss me. They became very pornographic and I began making him home movies. I genuinely trusted him with these films and photos.

Over time our relationship began to seriously crack. He became quiet. When he did talk he was demanding. He was no longer generous, and one day when he was very high he said he was hoping to break me and own me.

I began thinking he was cheating on me and grew super paranoid. I checked his laptop one day when he was in the other room and found emails that suggested I was being used for a sex bounty. He was selling my photos and films to a website. I was horrified and felt utterly sick.

I left him on the spot and drove the three hour trip back home, crying and wondering about taking my own life on the road. I knew I had been used but I was in denial. I believed that once he truly loved me. At the time I was so confused, and thought maybe I could get him to love me again.

I knew I now had a problem; I had a meth habit of around two grand a week, I had no job and no boyfriend.

I remember going home and feeling utter heartbreak and loss over him, yet still in love with him because he had been my 'Mr Perfect'. I was desperately holding onto the memories of him being nice, generous, funny, and taking care of my every need; a meth addicts dream.

A FAST EXIT ONTO A NEW LEVEL

I knew after our breakup that I had to go back to sex work straight away. It was awful; I knew what he did was wrong, yet I was still madly in love. I tried calling him, but he was refusing to pick up. I'd email him but get no response. I had no other choice; I had to get work.

I'd met a couple of women during my time at the brothel who were working privately. They had encouraged me to do it, but it felt so unsafe and scary to my mind. I decided to suck it up and be brave. I joined a website for advertising, and booked myself a room at one of the most expensive hotels in town. I wanted to attract wealthy businessmen rather than the gangs or roughies that often lurk around sex workers. I also knew I wanted to be in a place with lots of security cameras in case anything went wrong.

I took the key off the receptionist and began wheeling my little suitcase down the hall to the elevator. I rode to the top floor and headed down towards my suite. "Dear God, I ask for angels to protect me here tonight." I could feel my heart pumping with fear of the unknown and excitement all at the same time.

I opened the door; my eyes fell upon the most beautiful boutique room, with a large balcony overhanging the city below. I closed the door behind me and got out my handbag; I had to celebrate! My anxiety turned very rapidly into thrill and excitement. I sat on the bed with the view and began to get high straight away, loading up before my first client arrived. A feeling of independence, luxury and freedom suddenly washed over me. I knew I was going to love this. I knew I could support my drug habit now and I decided then that I would not be owned ever again, not by a boyfriend or a brothel. Unfortunately, I had no idea of the reality behind the star-studded curtain.

11

The Curtain

I lived in this star-studded curtain experience for many moments during my first year of being a private escort. Clients were high-paying businessmen. I bought exciting outfits and rented expensive hotels. We drank champagne, and I had regulars by the time my first month was out. This continued for the first few months. The illusion of a perfect life had blinded me to any possibility of danger, and my guard slowly dropped.

The first time I experienced the raw reality of what was behind this curtain was just a few months after I began. I received a phone call one day from a man in Auckland; he had seen my profile and wanted to invite me up to his home to discuss building a pornography site with him. I had already begun to make movies at work by myself and was sending them to America, so I thought he was linked in with that world.

I agreed at first, but in the final hour before I was due to leave, I had a gut-wrenching feeling that this was way too good to be true. I called him and cancelled my visit, but he said he already had a car sent for me and it would be there within the next couple of hours.

My boundaries had never been strong. I was a people pleaser and despite my guts screaming no, I didn't want to let anyone down, so I agreed.

I was picked up by a rough, old man with tattoos and an overhanging beer belly. He drove a dodgy beat-up white station wagon, and he pulled up at my home with a cigarette hanging from his mouth. I felt uneasy and nauseous as soon as I saw him. Yet again, I felt unable to say no because of my poor boundaries and wanting to 'not let anyone down.' I got into the car.

On the way to Auckland he told me how he had been part owner of brothels in my hometown but was now working in Auckland with the man I was scheduled to meet, to set up a pornography website. He said he was his driver.

We ended up chatting the whole way and I found myself easing up and feeling a bit more comfortable. However, if he claimed to be the driver of a high-flying player in the industry how come he looked like he did and drove what he did? I knew something was wrong.

We pulled into the house of the Aucklander. The house was a normal, suburban property in a local street; nothing special or hidden. The door opened and there stood a tall man in cowboy boots and slick, black hair, almost sounding like he was gay. There was something off about him, but I couldn't put my finger on it.

Inside I expected to find lots of other people who he had said were working on the project. Instead, it was just me and the two men. I wanted to get the meeting started straight away, but they laughed and said they wanted to get to know me first. They began pulling out drugs and alcohol and creating a smorgasbord on the table. The addict in my brain immediately switched on and I shared some meth with them.

We continued to chat, but every time I brought up the plan and the website, they would veer off down another track. I remember feeling increasingly nervous. I was drinking a small amount of wine and suddenly found myself in bed with the tall man who had been in the cowboy boots. I looked down and saw him inject something into my arm. I knew I was being drugged, and I felt immediately limp and helpless. Where was my phone? I tried to reach out for help, and that's when I saw the driver in the corner holding a video camera.

This went on for a while and then another man came in whom I hadn't seen before. He seemed to be a very well-dressed businessman. They appeared to be telling me that I liked to party and were acting very encouraging of my wasted state, as if I had done it to myself. I was really confused, but didn't fight back. Again, the people-pleasing side of me was kicking in and co-labouring with my inner addict.

The next thing I knew, I was in another house and the businessman was having his way with me. Then he brought me downstairs to a room full of other men. They handed me tabs of acid and I remember being too frightened to take it. I had taken acid before, plenty of times, but not in a situation like this.

One of the men told me that the teddy bear in the businessman's room had a camera inside and the eyes had been recording me. They said they were making a porn star out of me. I remember running away upstairs and curling up in a ball.

The businessman tried to have his way again, but this time I was shutting down. Hours passed as I lay clenched in a ball, cold fear pushing on me like a tonne of bricks, unable to move. I remember getting carried out and then found myself in a motel room on the outskirts of Auckland.

For the next 12 hours men would come and go while the driver waited outside or in the bathroom. I was so fearful for my life and sanity that I decided to make a run for it. Between clients, while the driver was in the bathroom, I got away and snuck to the reception. I had no sense of where I was or where my things were. My phone, drugs, camera and cigarettes had all been taken away.

I begged the receptionist to let me use her Facebook and messaged my friend from university days. The receptionist gave me the address of the motel and asked if I wanted to call the police. I shook my head; I knew police meant I could potentially be separated from meth. I waited in reception until, hours later, my friend pulled up.

I was distraught. She hadn't seen me in years and I know she hadn't seen me as a drug addict before. She drove me to the bus stop, gave me enough money for the fare and I got on the next bus back to my hometown, with nothing but the clothes on my back. The most frightening thing was thinking that they were going to come after me.

I tried to stay awake on the bus ride home. My brain was flicking in and out of reality and I was hungry for sleep, yet I was too scared to.

12

Torn

I arrived back in my home city. My mind was beginning to unravel from the drug cocktails, and the reality of what had happened kicked in. I had been kidnapped and raped and left with nothing. Yet who cared? Who had even known I'd gone to Auckland?

I went to Starbucks and asked to use someone's phone and contacted a close friend. She wasn't a working girl, but her boyfriend was my meth contact, so she and I had become quite good friends. She picked me up, and I went to stay at their place.

I decided I would never work again; my life was over. At her place, she, her boyfriend and I got high and smoked cigarettes outside to all hours of the night. I told them what had happened, but as we sat getting high, the reality of what had happened was becoming increasingly difficult to explain. I almost shrugged it off, not wanting to be a damper on them, not wanting to be a burden. I needed good company, and I really wanted to enjoy theirs.

I stayed with them for a few nights, smoking their meth with the money I had in my account but knowing it would run out. I woke up one day with the events buried in the back of my brain, but the reality of needing meth was looming toward me, so I decided to go back to work. But this time, I would be smarter and not accept ridiculous requests.

I knew I'd been made a fool of, and I knew they had those videos somewhere. I thought of returning to Auckland in the middle of the night just to burn their house down. Revenge.

Later on, as the months went by, I learned the guy's name. I did research on what brothel he was a partner in. I also learned he was awaiting sentencing for filming girls in their bookings, without permission, using secret cameras. When I heard that he'd got sentenced, I was overcome with relief and happiness. The pig had got his justice.

Life working as an escort had its ups and downs. The up days were sometimes back to back, day after day, night after night. I continued collecting clients who were businessmen or good-hearted young guys who wanted to have a good time with no strings attached. I worked out of hotels but eventually got myself a two storied apartment on the beach.

Some of them secretly recorded our sessions on their phones, and when I cottoned onto this, I decided to create sessions, that cost extra, with permission to film. This became my X factor, but it also became my downfall.

I got texts from strangers saying they enjoyed watching me, when I had no clue about it. I became paranoid. Where were these videos going? I knew technology was increasing, but so was my paranoia about being secretly filmed. I never minded videos, as long as I knew about them. One risk the clients liked to take was videoing without you knowing. It was called voyeurism, and it was a growing trend. This contributed massively to my paranoia.

One day, after a session, I got a text saying very particular things about me and the client; as if they had been watching the whole time. Had someone planted a secret bug? I was growing increasingly anxious after sessions and would scour the room for bugs afterwards, sometimes even burning the clothes I'd been in, in case they'd left a recording device on them.

The illusion of independence and security and wealth broke down a year and a half later. I was no longer awed and blinded by the star-studded curtain, I was behind it, deep within its grip.

One day I booked a client who I had screened over the phone, but upon arrival he was wearing his gang clothes and telling me he could own me if he wanted.

I hardly ever got high with clients. I kept my habit hidden to protect myself. However, that day I let my boundary slip as he pulled out stashes of meth and began to smoke in front of me. I joined him, telling him I never do this, and it was a one-off. He rubbished my comment and said he knew me, he knew what I was like, and that I was going to be owned very soon.

"Owned? No one owns me buddy. Jesus owns me though," I said proudly. I still maintained my prayers for safety often, and frequently claimed that Jesus looked after me. The man laughed and continue to get high.

Very soon after that, my regular clients began calling me, saying they were too afraid to visit anymore. When they would leave a gang-patched motorcyclist would follow them and eyeball them at the lights. They began to think I was owned and looked after by a gang, even though this was never the case. Unfortunately, they dropped off one by one, and the bookings I was getting turned out to be gang members.

I turned up in a very high-class hotel one time and went into a suite to find three patched members there, all wanting a turn. They would pay in meth, refusing to pay cash. I had no choice, because if I declined I knew I'd get raped but if I said yes, I would keep them happy.

Another time I was booked by a couple of guys who threatened to put me in a cage if I didn't do what they wanted. I remember being in this huge workshop alone with them, with the gang pad just down the road. But the most frightening part was the silver cage which they referred to was sitting in the middle of the room, waiting to hold me. I was lucky as I had a driver organised, that wasn't associated with the gang, to pick me up at a set time. I managed to please them and get out of there before getting locked up in the cage. I was petrified!

A little while later I was kicked out of the apartment I'd rented for six months because of the gang associates hanging around all the time. I knew then that things were starting to crack. I was losing most of my safe clients and now spent days and nights dodging gang members, becoming increasingly aware that I was about to get completely taken over and owned.

I was forced to go back into motels. Motels were affordable if I had a paying cash client. This was okay for a few months; I managed to get by. I would still book higher class places and seemed to still book regular cash paying clients, but this began to slowly dwindle down to only meth paying men.

It all happened so fast; one day I had several bookings only paying in meth, and I couldn't pay for my room. I didn't want to stay at my friend's place out of pride, so I walked the streets all night. The next day I got a booking, so I was in a motel again, but then, the day after that, I was out walking the streets again.

I would go to the clubs every Thursday, Friday and Saturday night. I would dance and drink and have a great time. I purposely never took a booking from a club because, for some reason, that was my safe spot. My home away from home. The barmen knew me and looked after me, and I looked after them by not using their bar as a pick-up place.

I'd often have a motel or hotel to go back to, but suddenly things were not working out, and I'd leave the clubs and continue walking the streets. I could fit everything I owned into my handbag. I would buy a new outfit and throw it out again after using it.

One day a client said he had been trying to call me but my phone was diverting. I took my mobile into a shop, and it was suggested that it had been diverted, so I had been missing calls. Had someone hacked my phone?

I felt desperately helpless. The gang was trying to own me all to themselves, threatening my regular clients, hacking my phone and now I was left to just work for meth and only take their bookings. I felt horribly trapped, yet not willing to give in.

I got a text message one day: "Come to our pad. We will put you on the block and then we will look after you. You won't have to walk the streets anymore."

I knew they were watching me. I had no money, my dignity was being sucked down the drain and the star-studded curtain of being a private escort was completely torn. I was standing naked in the reality of the underground world of prostitution.

13

The Cold, the Street and the Ugly

The gang continued to berate me through texts, asking me to come and visit them in exchange for a shower or a meal. They started saying they wouldn't even waste meth on me. It was heart-wrenching, and I felt incredibly trapped and broken.

I still managed to go to the nightclub on the weekends. One night I was leaving the club at 3am; it was closing, and everyone was going home. For some reason, I never hooked up with a guy outside of working, and during that stage, I felt too scared to go to another man's place that wasn't gang related. I knew I'd just invite punishment or trouble for him.

I walked from the club, but it was pouring with rain. I was shaking and cold, and had nowhere to go. I didn't want to bother a friend that I had, because I was ashamed of the pickle I had got myself in. Plus, I was scared that if I stopped anywhere, the gang would just come and take me away. They'd been threatening me for ages that if I escaped town or worked for anyone else, I'd get punished.

It was dark and pouring with rain, and suddenly I fell over onto the concrete. My knee felt like it had cracked open, and my phone fell in a puddle and split into two pieces. I couldn't get up; my knee was searing with pain. I crawled over to the concrete doorway of a closed shop. Then, as I realised how alone and broken I was, I began absolutely sobbing, my body wracked with physical and emotional pain.

Not only was I drenched in rain, but I was drenched in the feeling of being incredibly sad, broken and hurting, inside and out. A crater of loneliness was seeping into my soul. No-one knew I was out there, and through the pouring rain no-one could even hear me crying. I wasn't just crying though. I began wailing; really gut-wrenching crying as I sat, soaked, in the rain with absolutely no-one to help me and no chance of anyone hearing me.

I remember the breaking point was trying to find my cigarettes, only to have the rain soak them through. At that moment I felt like dying. I remember looking out into the dark sky and seeing the moon and knowing God was out there somewhere. "You have to help me" I sobbed.

It was about an hour later that I managed to hobble to the road. I waited for ages until a night-time taxi drove past. I waved him down. Crying I explained I had no money but I had to go to the hospital. I had hurt my knee. The taxi driver refused and drove off. Again, I waited for another one to pass, but again it was an hour later. I remember the hatred in my heart toward that taxi driver who chose to drive off instead of helping me; he had no idea what trouble I was in. I felt judged and ignored.

I finally got to the hospital. After the Xray, I was told it was just bruising, and I had to leave. I had nowhere to go, and by this time it was about 6 a.m.

"Can I wait in the foyer until daylight comes?" I asked.

The nurse shook her head. "We will have to get security to escort you out," she said.

I felt utterly helpless. I thought maybe in the hospital I'd find a bed for the night, even if it was just the safety of the waiting room.

It was Sunday morning now and buses didn't start until later. I was too sore to walk around and had nowhere to go, so I headed out and went and sat in the nearby cemetery.

Days on end, I continued walking around, occasionally picking up a booking I semi-trusted, to get enough money for my best friend, meth. I couldn't see, at that stage, that without meth the drama and pain in my life would cease.

I developed a cold one day. I kept walking along for a day or two.

I finally got a booking and ended up in a motel for the night. The next morning, I woke up with an unbearable ache in my ribs. Nothing untoward had happened and I certainly didn't remember pulling any muscles. It deepened and I felt like I couldn't breathe, plus I still couldn't shake the cold. I checked out of my motel and continued walking, knowing I was unable to work again and would be facing a few days on the street once more.

As I walked, it dawned on me that I was in trouble. I couldn't breathe; my chest was aching. I'd had that cold for a few days but now I had this deep ache in my ribs and I was struggling to breathe. I was physically weak and frail, but the pain on top made breathing near impossible.

At first, I thought it was a miracle when a van pulled over. I recognised a client of mine who I hadn't seen in a while. He had been kind and decent, but he too had gone away because of the drama surrounding my existence.

"Do you need a ride?" he asked. I started to cry and explained I was in pain and needed see a doctor. He agreed to take me to the hospital, but it would cost me. I couldn't believe it, but I had no choice. I remember getting in and agreeing, and through tears and flinches of pain, I had to do a booking in his van, just for a ride to the hospital. I'd had some damn lonely and degrading moments in my life as an escort, but I knew this was reaching the very bottom. The shame and disgrace of my homeless state was now staring at me, right there on the face of a man who once saw me in high-class hotels appearing sane and healthy. What was worse was the fact that the kind and caring man I once knew was revealing his true colours; unless I did a booking he wouldn't take me to hospital. The world I lived in was purely evil; the star-studded curtain had been a false illusion the entire time.

I got to the hospital and made my way to cardiology. As a kid I'd had two heart operations, and even when grown up I'd seen a cardiologist regularly. As far as I knew, he still worked there. I was right. He took one look at me and called up doctors immediately.

I was admitted instantly with pneumonia, but he said that was the least of my worries. I was malnourished and on the brink of a mental breakdown. I tried to explain the reality of the life I was living, trying not to be owned by a gang. Unfortunately it just got labelled as paranoia and they admitted me to the psychiatric ward.

14

A Doorway Through to Another Land

Upon hearing the doctors decide I was to be admitted to the psychiatric unit, I felt relieved. My fighting was over.

My parents met me at the hospital. I felt awkward seeing them, slightly embarrassed but trying my hardest to deny that meth was the reason I was like this; it was the gangs and the 'bullies' of the world that were driving me to despair.

I found hospital a nice break. I ate several times a day, slept a lot and chatted with other patients. I made some friends and spent time hanging around outside drinking hot chocolate, smoking cigarettes and sneaking off to get high at my friend's place or stoned with the other patients.

The best part of it was I felt safe. I had a bedroom with my own bathroom. I could lock it during the day and sit in there at night smoking cigarettes in the bathroom with the shower on so the steam would disguise the smoke. They gave me sleeping pills at night and I could just lounge around all day and eat if I wanted to. I would occasionally get paranoid that the gang knew I was in there, watching and waiting for me to return.

One day I was sitting inside my room and it dawned on me to try to escape. I was starting to run out of meth, despite saving benefit money to buy it and sneaking out to get it, and I was starting to crave the higher amounts I was used to.

I couldn't do any bookings, being in the hospital. The doctors were hesitant to release me, and I had been sectioned because of my inability to keep myself safe. Despite being legally sectioned there, I packed my bag and decided to climb the fence and walk off; not just into the city, but out of town. I was going to escape the hospital and then skip town when no-one was watching, to escape the gang.

I remember the thrill of rebellion and freedom, hope and adventure, rushing through my body as I walked off down the road. I was taking back control of my own life again. Why I hadn't thought of this before?

I hitchhiked up to Auckland with a trucker, making up stories on the way, of how I was independent and wanting a change of scenery; playing it cool as if I hadn't been living on the streets, a washed-up hooker who had been committed to an institution. In the hospital I had begun looking reasonably good again; my hair was back with colour and my clothes fit my body. I could almost pass as a normal human being.

In Auckland I joined a local nightclub where I could live and work at the same time; this solved my accommodation and money issues. It seemed okay for the first few days, but suddenly the national newspaper declared me as missing, put a full picture of

A DOORWAY THROUGH TO ANOTHER LAND

my face in it and stated that my safety and wellbeing were at risk. People began contacting the paper, saying they had seen me in Auckland.

Not only did it blow my new freedom of life away from the hospital, it pointed the gang to where I was. I panicked. Suddenly every client was a threat. But surely I'd not be found in a big city like Auckland?

One day I was walking down the main street, off to get something to eat. I was as high as a kite, having found a new dealer who was joined to the club. I came across a street evangelist, stopping people to share about Jesus. He was an older man, and passionate about his faith. I stopped to listen because something about his passion caught my attention. However, I felt sorry for him. I knew what being a Christian was like: God was aloof and the life was dull; full of good behaviour and living in a nice house with a picket fence. Life sucked, so why not party it up!

Having had my own experience of a 'religious life' I had quite the opinion about God, so I stopped to talk to him. He began to tell me about the love of God, that he had a plan for my life and I should repent and be saved. He put a huge emphasis on repentance and how my sin would lead to death. It was probably obvious I was high and a working girl. He continued talking about Jesus, and for some reason my opinions were put aside. I ended up sitting down to talk to him and told him of the dark life I was experiencing. He continued to try and persuade me to repent. He was telling me if I received Jesus into my life and repented for my sins I would be saved.

I can't be saved," I said.

He looked at me. "How come?" he asked.

"Well, let's say I receive Jesus now as my saviour, where would I go after this? I live and work in a brothel. Where would I sleep tonight? Who's going to help me to get off these drugs?" I said.

The man nodded; he could see my point.

"Unless I come home with you now, I can't be saved."

He nodded again. "At least let me pray for you?" he asked.

I shrugged, "Sure. Go for it."

I felt his hand on my shoulder and right there in the middle of Queen Street I let him pray for me. I think I closed my eyes, I don't remember, but it was the oddest lunch break I'd had for a while. However someone had reached out to me to try and help me. Most people at this stage in my life either judged me or, instead of reaching out to help me, wanted me put away.

15

Kidnapped

Shortly after, I came out of the brothel to find something to eat. I lived on one meal a day but usually found snacks of chocolate Kit Kats or smoothies to keep me going. I walked across the road to the petrol station to buy some snacks. An older man following me in, but I assumed he was a normal customer. He began talking loudly and acting oddly to the attendant, trying to draw my attention. "I just need a lady to spend the day with," he was saying. He caught my eye, and I mentioned I was free all day... but at a cost. He seemed elated.

"This is my lucky day. We'll go to the casino and gamble all day, drink all day and have a good time!" Plus, he promised to pay more than the club. I thought I'd struck gold.

We left the store together and went over to his car. He told me he wanted to get high first. "Why don't we book a room at the casino?" I asked.

He shook his head and turned on his car. "Nope... we have to go to my place." He sped away from the casino and continued on the highway, heading out towards South Auckland. My gut dropped as his behaviour became more erratic; I could tell he was already high.

"You know, I had another girl this morning," he jeered, "but I threw her off a bridge for being a little bitch! But I'm glad I found you. I feel like killing somebody today. Especially you.... you need to be punished, I've been told."

Suddenly, my whole body went into shock. I couldn't get out of the car; he was driving over 100km an hour!

"I'm just joking! No, we are going to have the best day ever. We just have to go home and get high... but I do feel like killing somebody," he said.

"Who? Why?"

"I don't know." He pulled out a gun from under his seat. "Why don't we go and shoot the local dairy owner." He was pulling into the suburbs of South Auckland. "Don't worry, I won't kill you. You're going to help me kill someone though... I just don't know who." He pulled into the driveway of a rundown flat. "C'mon get inside," he jested, and opened my door.

I was petrified! I could have run off then, but after seeing the gun, my mind and body were locked in fear.

"My neighbour's got 5 children. Why don't you go and invite them here to make muffins, and I'll kill them off one by one while you hold them down." He was acting jittery.

"No that's awful!"

He led me inside his house. There was a mattress in the lounge and a pile of girls' clothing in the corner. The kitchen was overrun with dirty dishes.

"I have to pee," I said, hoping desperately to sneak out the window.

"Good. I'm thirsty." He grabbed a cup and demanded I pee in the cup in front of him. I knew I was trapped. I'd been kidnapped, but was this a setup? Was this the punishment from the gang?

I did what he said and peed in the cup. Then, to my disgust, he took it from me, and keeping his eyes locked on me, he drank it. He took out his cell phone. "Call the dogs over, I've got her!" he said. The dogs? He has me?

Suddenly it was like a cold fear in me exploded into mania in my body. I screamed hysterically! He had taken my bag with drugs in it and cigarettes, but I didn't even care; I had to run. I bolted towards the door, fear stabbing through my skin like cold ice particles. My mind was in a manic state, with one goal: to escape! I could hear him coming after me!

Knowing he had a gun, I forced my shaky legs to bolt out the door, screaming for help. I ran down the suburban street towards the shops. I got out to the main road, not knowing if he was still behind me, and waved down a car, but I could see the woman had a baby-seat in the back. I ran past the car; I knew I was in real trouble and couldn't bring a mum into this shit.

The next car pulled over. A lady reached over and unlocked the back door for me and I leapt into the back seat. "Just go! He's got a gun!" I pulled myself down, screaming, and hid in the car. The lady sped off and was suddenly on the phone to the police. I couldn't stop screaming!

They instructed the lady to head to Manukau Police Station, but it seemed like forever. Cold fear was now dripping through my skin. I tried to explain what happened through sobs, and the lady tried desperately to convey to the police what I was saying. The police promised to meet us at the station as soon as we arrived.

We pulled up, and I ran to the doors, finally feeling like it was over, but they were locked! I banged on the window. I had the most awful, sickening feeling of needing help and it being denied, right in front of me. My mind was racing, thinking I was about to get tracked down and shot.

It was only a few moments, but it felt like the icy dread of forever. Two policemen finally opened the door and I remember screaming at them that they should have been there. Why had they locked the door?

The next I knew, I woke up in a police cell. What happened? Apparently, I'd passed out and was taken to a cell. I got up from the bed and started screaming for their attention.

"Why would you put me in this freaking cage after I'd been kidnapped," I sobbed.

The policeman unlocked the door and said he was taking me to the hospital. I still couldn't stop crying. "Just don't leave me alone," I begged.

He was really nice and caring, thankfully not treating me like a criminal. He said he would take me there and stay with me if he could. I felt safe for a moment.

He took me to Middlemore Hospital and put me in a single room surrounded by clear glass, outside the nurse's station. They immediately sedated me because I couldn't stop crying and screaming. I was in absolute shock and fear.

They gave me a sandwich. I ate half and decided to save half for the policeman, but before long, I fell asleep.

I woke up, hours later, alone. The policeman had left. I was even more distraught; I felt so vulnerable. What if the man had come to find me? Why had the police left?

I was sedated several times over the next few days and transferred to a normal ward.

The police eventually came back. I explained what had happened, and how he said he threw a girl off the bridge earlier that day. I had thought maybe it was a scare tactic, but to my horror, I found out he was telling the truth. That same morning a girl was admitted to the hospital after being thrown off a bridge!

I told the police about my experience, but was adamant not to do anything because I was petrified of repercussions. I lived a life locked in fear of punishment from the gang for leaving my hometown. Maybe he was involved in that? I felt sick with worry, with thoughts and possibilities running through my head constantly.

"Unfortunately, we can't release you. You're physically okay, but we're going to admit you to the psychiatric unit to be monitored and transferred back to your hometown. We know you were under a section of the hospital there," the doctors explained.

I was relieved in a way, because I knew I wouldn't have to be back out in Auckland on the street again. I knew I couldn't return to the brothel, because they had found me nearby. I would be easily tracked again. I wasn't sure if my paranoia about escaping ownership from the gang and being punished was real or the kidnapping was an isolated incident.

It was a lonely time, and I was terrified of being found. I spent all day and night lying on my bed. The feeling of fear was more compounding than the meth withdrawal that I was also experiencing.

I finally called my brother. He now lived in the South Island. We'd stopped speaking a year earlier because my lifestyle had become too much for him. I told him what had happened, and that I was in the hospital.

"Okay, come home now. It's got to be over for you," he said.

I agreed. In my soul, I knew it was over. It had to be over.

"Come down here and I'll sort you out. You can get off everything and start a new life. I'll help ya."

"Okay. I will. I've got to get out of hospital first. I'm being sent from Auckland back to my home hospital, but when I get out, I'll come down. Okay? It's over. I promise."

I felt deep in my heart that I was being honest and truthful. I wanted it to be over. I had just experienced a near-death experience, again. It was enough to make me want to cut ties with the sex industry altogether. My first year had been an illusion of false promises, control, power, money, and being idolized. Now the reality of being owned, living in fear, and being a slave to addiction was my daily grinding reality.

16

Inside-out

My brother had offered for me to go to the South Island and live with his family. I'd get clean and start a new life. But the addict in me rose and began taking over. I started thinking about meth again; recalling the good days where it had been hassle free. I'd been wanted, idolised, and had some control. Maybe I could get back to that.

Meth is like a violent domestic relationship; you look back at the good times and can't imagine your life without that person. The pain and reality are hidden behind the false promise of 'that won't happen again'.

Somewhere deep inside me, I knew I was a tragic, broken mess. I knew that if I went to my brother's, I might have a breakdown or disrupt his family.

Part of me really wanted meth again. Now I was thinking about being released, the option to use was strong. But although part of me knew I was wrong, I couldn't imagine settling into a family unit right now.

I was transferred to the mental health unit in Auckland, and I spent the few days in bed alone, being monitored by nurses through the night and day. It was awful.

I was finally escorted in a van, with hospital security, back to my hometown. I remember the guards being smokers, and being so relieved whenever we stopped, because they'd share their cigarettes with me. I was only wearing the hospital gown because I'd lost all my other belongings at the man's home and left them there when I escaped. The one outfit I'd been wearing, I had thrown away in disgust because of the memories it held.

They transferred me to my hometown hospital, but instead of letting me stay in the mental-health ward, they delivered me to IPC, the Intense Psychiatric Care unit. This was a separate wing from the mental health ward.

They drove into the garage and locked the doors before I even got out of the van. They led me, like a prisoner, down the hall to a large cell. It held a bed with a plastic mattress, and a barred window.

"Wait here."

"What? No way! I don't need to be here! What have I done wrong?" I became distraught and began swearing and kicking at the guards, but I was physically restrained and made to wait.

I waited at least an hour before the doctors came in with a lawyer. They didn't even ask me questions, but instead read me my rights. I was recommitted as a patient.

They transferred me from the large cell to a smaller one. It was part of five other cells off an open lounge. There was an outdoor area fully enclosed by metal gates and bars.

I was furious! I was sick of being trapped, sick of not being able to smoke, sick of being owned. For me, this was just another experience of having no control and being subjected to fear.

The unit was exactly like a small jail: cells, metal toilets, bars. The worst part about it was the patients. They were all criminally insane or a major risk to themselves or others.

I isolated myself in my cell, refusing to eat or drink for the first day or so. I don't know if I was being manipulative or if I was genuinely sad about the situation. I felt I was owned, all over again, but this time it was by the government. I wasn't sure which felt worse, gangs or government. I thought maybe the government, because at least on the streets, I could smoke and do what I wanted to some extent.

I recognised a few nurses from my previous stay in the hospital. They genuinely tried to help me by being nice. I never kicked up for them.

I hated being there, and they knew it. I would not hurt anyone else, and I didn't think I'd hurt myself either. The doctors said it was because I was at risk of being hurt and was needing monitoring. I felt it was just their way of punishing me for my escape last time.

I watched a few other patients swearing at the nurses and trying to punch them. Despite my situation, I liked the nurses and doctors, so I didn't even make a fuss, plus I was trying to get out on good behaviour.

I made one friend, an old lady who had tried to kill herself multiple times. She was the only one in the unit who was not mentally insane and dangerous. She loved food and was quite overweight. She had stashes of chocolate brought in for her, and endless amounts of lollies. The food was so bland in the unit that she would often share her chocolate, and that became one of the few things I'd eat.

Our meals were brought to us on a huge, rolling dinner wagon, one tray stacked upon the other. We were then called from our cells to the dining room. It was flooded with fluorescent light that gave me blinding headaches, with no windows except one to a hallway where the security nurses watched us eat. We had three tables to choose from, so there was never a chance of sitting alone.

The nurse-guards would call our name and we would collect our tray. Then they'd stand at the locked door or on the other side of the window and wait, watching us eat until we had finished. I often just gave my food away. It was usually mashed potato made from a packet, cold green beans, and a piece of meat that was probably not meat at all. It was disgusting.

I made alliances by giving away my meals. "You can have my meal tonight, if you stop fucking me off," I'd say, especially to the guys that who had lurked around my cell door. Food was an effective bartering system.

One day, I came into my cell from the TV room and found a guy ferreting through my stuff. The only thing I owned was a fruit collection I was saving from my meals, and the hospital toiletries. I immediately began to defend myself. I grabbed my toothbrush and threatened to stab him. I knew I'd have no chance, but the commotion was enough to get the nurse-guards in to take him away. He never did that again. I was small, but I wanted them to know I wasn't to be messed with. I wasn't trying to be tough, but I had learnt quickly that I had to appear tough and crazy to look after myself.

My parents began to visit, but I refused to see them. They'd speak with the doctors and then I'd refuse to visit them, staying in my cell or the TV room.

I was in the unit for six weeks, day in and day out, with nothing to look forward to, not even food. I could hardly stay in the TV room because I hated being around the other patients.

Finally, one day I was released into the mental health wing. They had trusted enough me to be on that side of the hospital. I could walk freely outside to have cigarettes.

Once over the other side, the first few days were like heaven. I had better food, and I was allowed to just have ice-cream or mashed pumpkin if I wanted.

There were more patients willing to swap food here. Meal times were way more fun because we would all sit and laugh and chat; most of the people could hold reasonable conversations.

There were people from all walks of life; mostly suicide attempts or medication errors had led people to be in the ward, as well as a few people from the streets or with chronic mental health disorders. I will never forget the comradery we all had together.

They became like a tightknit family for me, something I was yearning for and missing. They were easier to talk to, less criminally insane and much safer. I'd known a lot of them from when I was previously admitted. They too had left and returned.

I'd made a name for myself, escaping and ending up in the newspaper. I laughed it off with the others, but they didn't know the shame of the ordeal, or what it had cost me. I received the sickness benefit while I was in there and I'd saved enough money to buy myself cigarettes. This was the only thing I looked forward to.

17

Fizz

I'd been off meth now for two months; it was the first time in two years I'd had a sober stint this long. I was getting healthier, but still had the mind-set that I was a prostitute. I knew I was going to need to get back out there if I wanted my friend back in my life. I still believed meth had helped me become a better person. I started thinking this all through.

Maybe I could just hide it better and get in less trouble with the gangs. Maybe I could get back to how it used to be; working in hotels and only seeing selected businessmen? I had been so broken and cut by now though, that the thought of trying one more time in that world was almost too much. Was my life over? I knew nothing else outside of being a prostitute.

I realised one day that after everything I'd gone through, I didn't want to go back. Yet what else was there? Inside myself, I must have been disconnecting from life, bit by bit. The novelty of being in the open ward was wearing very thin, and there seemed no way I could get off the section soon, so as to be legally allowed to leave.

One morning, I decided I would end my life. I was done. I felt relief after making that decision. I took a plastic bag and turned the shower on, then I sat underneath and tied the bag over my head. I remember feeling sad; sad that it was all over, sad for the tragic end my prostitute's life was coming to. I felt like the glitz and glamour was too far gone now. The reality and brutality of gangs and random kidnappings had interrupted and murdered any chance of a good, successful life as a prostitute. I remember just an overwhelming feeling of being so sorry for myself.

I sat there under the shower, breathing in, breathing out, feeling the air escape bit by bit and my lungs getting tighter. Then I felt pressure in my head... then everything went black.

A little later I came to, with doctors and nurses around me, bringing me back to the world. I cried when I came to, and felt a massive headache and a bit of confusion. I thought for sure I'd be sent back to IPC lockup. However, I was given the grace I needed to talk through why I'd done it, and be given hope. Instead of being punished, the nurses allowed me to just relax and gain strength for life again. I have no idea why they didn't send me back to lock-up.

I stayed in the hospital for another couple of weeks, improving with medication and regular chats with the nurses. I decided I wanted to go back out there and try again.

They released me from the hospital with just enough money to buy a cheap phone. I contacted a client, booked a room and was straight back into business. For a few days, I felt incredibly powerful and happy. I got more meth and started the cycle all over again. I hit it as hard as I had ever, even though I'd had a brief break while in hospital.

I ignored the heartache I was causing my family, as they'd hoped that when I got released, I'd live with my brother, but I knew I wasn't ready. I'd be too much of a mess for him and his family. I smoked meth as much, if not more, than I had before.

I felt a bit jaded one morning. I'd been up all night smoking with a friend; walking around my room, smoking, chatting, and feeling free. My friend left in the early hours of the morning and I was feeling really tired. I walked across the kitchen to get a coffee. I went to pick up the coffee jar when a jolt ran through my body! The coffee slipped from my hands and I felt my body being slammed to the ground as though a mighty force pushed me down. I felt my brain inside my head fizz out.

Shocked and confused at what happened, I managed to get up. I attempted to grab the bench again for stability, but this time a more powerful jolt hit me and a longer, deeper fizz circuited through my brain. I felt my body being slammed onto the concrete floor. I cried out in shock.

Although still conscious, it dawned on me that I was having a seizure. I began sobbing. I was too scared to get up. I was all alone and confused. I dragged myself to the phone, dreading the decision I had to make.

"Dad," I cried down the phone, "my brain went fizz and I can't move properly!"

I cried, but Dad remained calm but assertive. Where was I? Had I been smoking meth?

Then I heard Mum lose it in the background. She was shouting and upset, because I'd thrown away my opportunity to get clean. On top of my hysterics and fear, I was now being shut out of any hope of family connection.

But still my dad came over in his little red car, helped me get off the floor and took me to the hospital.

The doctors were adamant not to give me an MRI, despite my persistence, because they knew it was meth related. They explained I had used after being dry for a short period and it had triggered a small seizure.

I was distraught. My best friend, meth, nearly killed me. My options were to quit, but what was the point of life if I quit?

Dad dropped me back to my temporary accommodation. As I pulled up in Dad's car, the manager of the unit was waiting for me outside. "You were up all night and we suspect you're using drugs. This is a no drug zone. We're kicking you out!" she said.

"I just had a seizure and had to go to hospital! I just got home. You can't kick me out. I have nowhere to go!" I cried.

She shook her head. "Not my problem." Dad confirmed that I wasn't allowed home either.

I went inside and packed up the few belongings I had. My only option was to go to my friend's place, but I knew I couldn't stay there. I used the rest of my money to buy more meth and promised myself I'd be moderate.

I'd just got kicked out of my accommodation, I hadn't booked any clients, I wasn't allowed back home and I had been spending too much time getting high instead of working. I decided the best solution was to join a brothel again.

I started working there, knowing that in that same city I'd been warned not to work for anyone else or I'd be murdered. Despite that, I felt I had no choice. Perhaps I could hide out here? The gang had left me alone since I'd been in and out of hospital. Maybe it was over, and I could get on with my life.

This lasted just two weeks.

18

Paranoia and Delivery

One day, someone wanting a private booking messaged me. I replied, asking for some details. "How many of us can you handle?" was the reply.

I was cautious, and despite my working adventures going horribly wrong, I was still naïve. I inquired some more.

"It's time to put you on the block. We know where you're working, and you belong to us. If you want our protection, you'll have to come on the block."

Fear set in; I'd been busted. I immediately knew I couldn't work there anymore. I replied "No."

I had a working friend who had experienced the block (gang rape) once, and could never again work. She had to have operations to repair the damage.

Still, the texts kept coming in, pressuring me to come down to the pad.

PARANOIA AND DELIVERY

Paranoia and fear set in, like the old concrete slab I had lived under for months. This time, I felt I was out of options. I quit the brothel and began walking the streets; too scared to stop, too scared to book a motel or a private client. The texts became increasingly harassing. I continued walking the streets, day in and day out. I'd sit in McDonalds at night time, or I'd sit in open doorways under security cameras. During the day I'd walk and walk, or sit in the park. I was running out of meth and money.

Then they began following me on their bikes. I wasn't sure if they were intimidating me or just out and about. "Come on, give it up... we'll give you a bit of meth," they'd say. It was tempting.

I began negotiating; could it not be at the pad? Could they promise not to hurt me?

"Sure... but this is what we want to do to you..." They would name exactly what they were planning to do, and it sent chills down my spine. I was growing hungrier by the day and my weight was plummeting.

"I want money, meth and a meal," I texted back.

"Meth, and maybe fish and chips, ha-ha," was the reply.

"No." I couldn't do it. I felt like the most alone, isolated girl in the entire world. The texts would come in once or twice a day. It was the ultimate standoff, but I felt increasingly backed into a corner.

I began riding the bus during the day, using one concession, just staying on as long as I could. One day I refused to get off because of where the bus stopped. It had stopped out in the industrial zone at the bus depot and the driver refused to take me further. I sat there and cried and swore at the driver, but refused to explain what was going on. I felt no one believed me. He threatened to call the police, so I got off.

It was raining quite hard, so I walked a couple of hours to the mall. I got to the mall and tried to tidy myself up in the bathroom. Again, another text, "It's time."

I threw my phone in the rubbish, snapping the sim and pouring water all over it and slamming the lid. I felt I couldn't escape them, even without my phone.

I stayed in the mall until closing time. It was around midnight and all the people had gone back to their families, back to their homes. I sat in a chair outside the closed shops, feeling safe in the wide-open space of the mall, but I knew it wouldn't last.

The security guard approached me. "It's time to go," he said.

I shook my head; it was dark outside. I was refusing to leave. "I'm hiding."

I eventually broke and explained that I was a working girl, and I was being targeted. He was genuinely interested then, and I felt he believed me.

"Okay. I'm going to take you to the police," he said.

I shook my head. "They can't help me."

I had been there once before, while walking the streets day in and day out for two weeks. One night it was raining, and I went there and asked to be put in a cell. I briefly explained my situation, but they told me to fuck off and that I was a meth head. I felt no alliance with them anyway, as they knew who I was and they hated my lifestyle.

"I need to go to the hospital," I said. The security guard agreed.

I was petrified as we left into the carpark and shocked to see one of the gang members sitting on his motorbike under a street lamp in the mall car park, just waiting.

"See!" I sobbed, "I knew he was waiting for me." I knew it wasn't paranoia, and I knew then I could prove it.

The guard rushed me to the hospital and dropped me at the emergency room. I ran in. "I'm being targeted!" I cried.

I gave my name, and the nurse pulled up my records. Suddenly, the roaring sound of the motorcycle pulled up outside the waiting room, revving his engine before speeding off. I broke down, shaking in fear.

"See! You didn't believe me... you didn't believe me," I sobbed.

The nurse rushed me through and they put me in the safety of an isolation room. The doctors came and we explained my situation to them. This time, they took me seriously and instead of blaming it on paranoia, they genuinely recognised my need for safety.

"We are going to put you back in IPC," they said.

I didn't care at that stage; my meth was gone, I was backed into a corner and it was all over. It was all gone. Finally, I could see that the life I had tried to build up again was just an illusion. It was never going to work. Meth was like a magnet to the gangs, and being a single person with no place to live I was an easy target.

I agreed, and they took me by car to the IPC unit.

During my first few days there, I lay in the cold, firm cell bed, refusing to drink water or eat. I knew I was sick, malnourished, and dehydrated, but most of all, I was exhausted. I had walked the streets for two weeks, trying to stay safe and in public view. I needed sleep and rest. I felt safe in lock-up.

It was a small unit, and I knew the doctors. I could even tolerate the dreary days as the hours dragged by.

I slowly began to come out of the room into the open area, eating food and watching TV. The doctors saw me once a week, and after a few weeks they decided I'd be court sectioned, either to a rehab or to my parents.

The court date was set, and a lawyer, who I'd never even met, read my case to the judge. They decided I wasn't safe looking after myself, trusted out in the community or even in the open section of the mental health ward. I was to be sectioned at my parents' address for six months on a community order, and if that didn't work, I was scheduled for rehab.

Leaving the IPC after nearly 6 weeks was frightening. I didn't want to go back to the world. What if I was shot, killed, or kidnapped? I was an open target. What if they knew where my parents' home was?

Dad took me home. Mum was reluctant, but had rolled up her sleeves to offer me a second chance, or possibly a fifteenth. The amount of times I had been clean and then cracked was painful for my family.

Mum and Dad had a beautiful home in a nice area, a fridge stocked with wholesome meals; no packet mashed potato, and no cold corn beef or string beans that wilted on your plate. Mum had huge soft sofas, and I had a very nice, tidy, warm bedroom.

I was so relieved to be there; out of the stark cold of IPC, with no crazy people to hassle me, and food I could gloriously feast on. I could smoke my cigarettes, I could keep warm and I could have a shower without the water automatically shutting off after two minutes. The comforts of my new home were like cushions for my soul.

I felt so warm and happy, for the first couple of days. However, the world was literally just outside my front door. The sounds of memories echoed in my mind; the reality that meth was just down the road. There were no window bars, no cell, nothing other than my parents' desire and will was actually keeping me away.

I began thinking about meth again; how close it was, how easy it would be; I could slip out and get some. But then I remembered the pain of emptiness and fear and isolation that it left me with.

The reality dawned on me that meth wasn't my best friend. It promised me everything; highs, good times, freedom, thin body, men wanting me, independence... but all it actually delivered was fear, isolation, and a constant experience of running away from somebody or something. The good times it promised were overshadowed by the dark reality, that eventually would lead to my death. I had come too close to that reality. Like a violent domestic relationship, it promised good times, so I'd return, time and time again. But each time, the good times only lasted a few days. Then I'd be left, beaten and alone, on the streets. Beaten by paranoia and alone because the illusion of prostitution fell away once men went back to their own families. They never even knew my real name.

19

Purchased

This tug of war became a battle in my mind that I was desperate to win. I knew the reality now that life on meth brought, the truth that it really did steal, kill and destroy. However, I could hear it calling me.

I was in my bedroom just a few days after my return to my parents' home. The battle inside was huge, and I was devastated that I couldn't win it. I had prayed to God throughout my time as a prostitute, sporadically at times, for safety, but even though my prayers shot up to a God I knew existed somewhere, he was never real in my heart or in my awareness.

"God. If you're out there, I really need help. Can you take this addiction away from me?" I knew I had nothing left; nothing to live for and no real hope of staying free, no matter how much I thought I wanted it.

As I sat there in my room I became aware of a peace that began flowing softly in and around me. I became aware that this peace was holy, it was beautiful. I hadn't actually known this peace. Ever.

It was soft and pure, and I knew instantly God had heard my prayer. The peace that filled up my room was tangible.

I quickly found the Bible I'd always owned. I pulled it out and flipped it open to a random page. Isaiah 42:7 *'You will free the captives from prisons, releasing those who sit in dark dungeons.'*

Suddenly it was like a white light of purity flooded inside of me! The peace flooded my soul, spirit and body, and I became aware instantly that I had just been set free from methamphetamine. I sat there reading those words and I began to cry. I had just been released from IPC, where I had spent my time sitting in that dungeon of a cell, but inside I knew that for the last two years I had been a captive of meth, alone in its dungeon, blind to the fact that it was a prison of torture.

For a long time, I sat in my bedroom and soaked in the presence of God, the one who I had called out to for help. He was showing himself to be very real to me. I knew it was God showing up in my room, telling me he was there, because the peace surrounding me was something I had never known. In my strongest, happiest day as a meth user I couldn't even imagine a peace like this. It was surreal! I had just prayed, and God was showing me he was there. With me... a prostitute!

I continued to stay at my parents' home. I would take short, timed walks around the block, walking my parents' dog. It was on those walks that I began talking to God, believing he was with me.

My parents had decided to move down to the South Island, where my brother and sister were. My brother and sister were very reluctant to even have me in the South Island, let alone be part of the family, so my family decided that I should to go to a rehab until I'd proven myself enough to fit back into the family.

I was half-hearted towards the rehab. I knew it would take a while for my family to accept me back into their trust again, but I was sure I was over rehabs. I wanted something different; I wanted true, powerful change. I was hungry for a freedom I didn't know existed but I'd dreamed of. Rehab had usually just offered me a survivor mentality and an identity as a recovered addict. There was something stale about that, and I knew I was hungering for fresh bread. Something in me knew God was offering it. Still, I went to rehab.

My first couple of days in I knew it was a step backwards. The cravings returned and I found it hard to connect again with God. I felt like I was slipping backwards inside, and I began to think about running away. I didn't like the environment or the lady running it. Something in me just knew it would actually do more harm than good.

I'd also been imprisoned, locked up, mentally and physically for the last two years, either by addiction or by the hospital. The last place I wanted to be was confined to rehab. God had spoken directly to me through his word; I was to be released from a dark dungeon, captive no more. Somehow being in rehab didn't fit with that promise.

I explained myself to the manager and packed my bags quickly; I had made up my mind and there was nothing stopping me.

Part of me wondered if actually having the power to choose and walk out was more exhilarating than anything. I had previously been owned and locked away. Here I could choose to stay or go. But I knew I had to leave. It wasn't just about the freedom to choose; I was choosing freedom from ever being in a dark dungeon again!

I knew my parents were still staying in town, part of the way on their move to the South Island. I walked from the rehab into town and found the motel. They were still sleeping; it was before 9am.

I arrived at the motel and banged at the window and the door. I could hear groans of frustration and disbelief as my mother recognised my voice. Finally, Dad shuffled to the front door.

"I want to come with you, please! I need to change. I can't stay here. Please!" I marched into the room and began pacing up and down, desperate to convince them not to lock me up again.

Mum was nearly in tears. She looked shattered by my outburst. "Prove it. Throw away your cigarettes," she challenged.

I hesitated only a moment, but I knew I had to give this everything I had. I threw them in the bin under the counter, my heart pounding. This was actually huge; alongside meth, cigarettes were my next best friend. I dreamed of them just as often as meth when I was locked up.

"See. Please?" I was looking into my mother's worn, tired face. Despite my encounter with God and his promise to release me from this dark dungeon, I hadn't told my parents of my new faith. They would think it was a joke.

Mum was exhausted; my whole family was. However, she reluctantly agreed, but with firm boundaries in place... no drug talk, no dressing like a prostitute, no swearing, no complaining, no smoking and no glorifying past behaviour.

I could go!

I felt free! Even though I was under a six-month community order, being with my family was more freedom than a rehab or hospital could ever offer.

Something about being released from a dark dungeon resonated, not just in my spirit, but it demanded reflection in my physical environment.

The only barrier was accommodation. My parents were to live with my sister and her husband until they bought a house, but she was refusing to talk to me, let alone see me. However, she lived next door to Mum and Dads' close friends, who had a small sleep-out converted from a shed in their backyard.

Everyone finally agreed; I could live in the shed, with strict instructions to not communicate with my sister until she was ready. I had let my sister down so many times. It had hurt her beyond description when I had used drugs and chosen a life of prostitution.

20

Greener Grass Still Needs Mowing

Moving down south was surreal. I could almost physically feel the cloak of paranoia and the memories of fear and drugs fall off me as I sailed across the ocean from the North Island to the South. It was a new beginning. No one knew me under any other name, apart from Marie. I hadn't been called Marie in two years. In fact, I felt I was arriving in a raw form of myself; no shadow of the past lingered with me. I had my Bible in my bag and a few pieces of clothing Mum and Dad had bought from Kmart, and that's it.

Mum and Dad dropped me off at their neighbours. I knew this couple from when I was a child. They were a joyful, non-judgemental couple, perhaps oblivious to my misdemeanours. They welcomed me like I'd done nothing wrong, buying me sushi for dinner, treating me as if they had no clue what I'd been up to or where I had been in the last two years. They said grace before the meal and talked about their church life and their life in the South

Island. I could use their mail box as my postal address; they had no idea about the daily bills I would begin to receive shortly.

The shed was small but warm. It had a lamp, a stand-up cupboard and a television. Inside I was alone; free but also safe.

I had either been in a small room, locked up and owned by the government, or I'd been taunted by gangs and on the street. Here I was safe. Not owned, free. Yet I had a roof over my head, and it wasn't a hospital roof! Praise God, I could already see that I was being released from the dark dungeon.

I lay in my bedroom with nothing but the Bible to read and I was almost bored.

I flicked on the television but nearly every advertisement, TV show or even the background music somehow reminded me of my past. I felt like the songs, the language, the clothes, and the people were entrenched with memories. It made me think about my time in the pornography world... I could have made it big... I almost did.

Suddenly I switched the TV off. I have to stay free! I can't think like that! I grabbed my Bible; God had shown himself to me, and I was going to find him again. If this person, Jesus, has died to set me free and apparently is claiming he can walk me out of this shit, then I must find out everything I can about this!

I opened the Bible and read Romans 12.2. It says, *'Don't copy the behaviour and customs of this world, but let God transform you into a new person by changing the way you think'*. I paused and thought about that. If I copied the behaviour and customs of this world, I'd be considered to be doing really well, yet God wanted me to aim higher... and have a new way of thinking! How could that be? My mind was still riddled with filthy thoughts and attitudes, about myself, sex and the world. How would I ever get my mind out of the gutter? Even if I managed to think simply for a moment, I almost always fell back into thinking about my past.

"God, how do I change my thinking? My mind is filthy!" I began to chat with him like that, as if he was right there in my room, and again, I felt a sense of peace around me; thick and still.

I turned the pages and read Ephesians 5.26: *'to make her holy and clean, washed by the cleansing of God's word'*. Oh... so the more I read the Bible the more I'd be cleansed? Seriously, I'm going to have to never, ever stop reading the Bible!

It was a frustrating time over the next couple of weeks. I would put the Bible down, go do my washing or make some food, maybe go for a walk with my parents or even just rest, but thoughts of my past, images of sex and vanity would creep in. It was a constant battle I could never win.

I cried out to God in frustration one day, so exhausted from trying and failing. My mind was disgusting! How can I change?

As I cried to God about this, crying on my bed and getting angry that his promises were almost too hard to grab hold of, too unrealistic, I read *"For you do not fight against flesh and blood enemies, but against evil rulers and authorities of the unseen world."* Ephesians 6.12. Then this thought popped into my head, "You're not fighting against a physical meth pipe or someone here reminding you about prostitution. It's spiritual." Then I read 2 Samuel 22.35: *'For he trains my hands for battle, so that my arms can bend a bronze bow.'*

"Really God, you're going to train me to fight and to win?" I could see it clearly now. I was fighting a spiritual battle of addiction, but unlike every other fight I'd ever had in my life, this one was a fight I was going to win. The almighty God was showing me, as I talked with him and turned to read the Bible, that I was going to win this fight of addiction.

But how?

A few days later, I was recommended a book by Bill Subritzky. It was about spiritual warfare. As a child of God, adopted into God's family since I believed in Jesus, I was now equipped with the name of Jesus and the power of his name as a weapon to use in any spiritual battle.

Spiritual battles were all around me at first. Jesus had given me freedom, but the enemy was wanting me addicted again. He was using thoughts, temptations, music, TV, memories and fear to entice me back again. I knew I had been set free from the cage of prostitution, but I had to walk out of it.

Jesus Christ had set me free. He'd unlocked me on the day I first cried out to him. But now I was being taught how to walk out of the prison free, paid for by the blood of Jesus.

Every time I woke up in the morning, the first thought I'd often have was a memory of waking up in hotels and smoking meth. It used to be my favourite time of the day, before clients. I had it all to myself and I'd get myself jacked up before the day. Now, instead of fighting that urge to use, and feeling like a failure because I was tempted, and then crying about it all before I got up for the day, I began using the name of Jesus, recognising the temptation as a spiritual attack.

"In the name of Jesus, I command you spirit of addiction to leave!"

Then I read in the Bible in Hebrews 4.12 that the word of God is like a sword in our hand. I would then start speaking out the word of God, the Bible verses that God had showed me, and imagined them to be like a powerful sword cutting through the temptation.

It really was astounding; as soon as I physically spoke the name of Jesus and a Bible verse, I would be filled with peace! My brain would slow to a calm state and I knew I had won that battle. For the first time in my life I was winning. I was so encouraged when I read verses that promised me I would be the head and not the tail. I knew it was possible! I could see it happening right before me.

Soon, I was thinking about God the moment I woke up. I'd pray for my family, and for myself to get a normal job. I'd even pray that God would teach me more about himself and this life he was offering me. I loved the Bible; I took it everywhere with me. It became my daily bread and I was hungry for it. I knew God was doing a deep work.

I'd begun sharing with my parents about what was happening. They were supportive, but still hesitant. My brother and sister thought it was just another pretended hope that I was giving them; that it would be a passing thing and I'd soon be gone.

I couldn't deny the encounters I'd had with God though. I could sense his physical presence in my room. I could feel a thick peace around me. The more I read the Bible, the more I learned about the promises that God has, for those who believe in his son Jesus. The deep freedom that was unlocking my heart and soul was something I can't even put into words. It just happened bit by bit.

I struggled through the walking out process though, despite God's peace and presence. There were memories and desires in me that I had to put to death.

One day I was standing in line to get an ice-cream. Two thin girls came in looking careless, wild, and dressed like I used to dress. Something in me burned like a jealous rage, almost angry I wasn't like that anymore. Here I was waiting to get an ice-cream and probably on my way to getting fat. No one knew my name anymore, like they used to. I wasn't being idolised anymore, and I was no longer a sex symbol. I almost began to resent my situation.

Then a thought popped into my mind, "You're no longer a sex symbol. You are wife material." Wow! The process of transformation was highlighted there in front of me, and I quickly recalled the scripture in Philippians 3.8: *'I consider all things worthless compared to gaining Christ.'*

I stood in that line and thanked God for what he had brought me out of. I remembered the lies that kind of life holds; it looks good but I knew the painful reality. God, on the other hand, had promised not to harm me or make me feel trapped. He promised to provide for me, so I didn't have to worry. He promised to adopt me into his family, so I never had to be lonely. He promised to set me free so I never had to be addicted. All the things I'd longed for in the life and world of the sex industry, God was offering me.

21

Paying Up

I first got into the sex industry because of the independence it offered me. I would earn more than I could dream of. The money would allow me to buy drugs. That's what I believed. It was true to a point. I would earn $800 or $1000 a night, I would then go and buy drugs for myself and my boyfriend. I'd buy cigarettes, alcohol, pay the rent and then it would be gone. I'd have to do that all over again the next night. I would earn just enough to have a good time. I would repeat that same process night after night, day after day. I wasn't independent; I was fully dependent on a false sense of freedom.

I began to get bills coming in the mail now. I was in my new life but my old life caught up with me. There were bills from debt collectors, from unpaid lawyer's bills, credit cards I had tacked up, and police fines. Daily, I would get more bills.

I started thinking about the money I'd earned in the sex industry and the money I'd wasted on drugs. How could I have earned so much yet still have so much debt? It didn't make sense. Maybe I should go back to work for one more night and pay the bills; surely God wouldn't mind?

I turned and opened my Bible, frustrated at the debt but unable to pay it; following Jesus but having my past follow me. 1 Timothy 6.17 told me, *"Teach those who are rich in this world not to be proud, nor to trust in their money, but in the living God, who richly gives us all we need for our enjoyment."* Seriously? I could feel the Spirit of God in me bringing peace, shifting my thoughts to fix them on this promise. I have to consider everything worthless compared to knowing Christ. I can't turn away to prostitution just to earn money to pay off my bills. I have to trust God, that he will help me!

I remember one day my toothbrush failing on me, my sandal broke, I'd received another bill in the mail and I was on the government benefit. I couldn't even afford a toothbrush, yet here was God telling me not to worry; that he will provide. I cried a lot that day, feeling defeated by the reality of society, bills, not being able to afford a toothbrush, living in a shed and not having a normal job. Would or could God seriously help me?

After a couple of months of this, time was becoming torturous. I would spend time reading my Bible and praying, but I also spent a lot of time crying and fighting temptation. I got into exercise; I walked a lot and rode a borrowed bike. I had no friends and I was deadly lonely.

Finally, with some courage, I applied for a job at a café. I didn't mention any of my past, I simply mentioned I had been travelling and had come to the South Island with my family. It was partly true; I did do a lot of travelling overseas and within the sex industry, and I also travelled to and from hospital a lot!

To my surprise I got the job. It was one of the nicest cafes in the city and I had been chosen to work there. Yay! I was so grateful to God, but I was as nervous as anything. It was my first real job out of the sex industry. How could I pull this off; one of the nicest cafes in the city with respectable staff and an expectation to make awesome coffee for wealthy people?

I remember my first day; I was full of nerves but also determined to prove myself. They had no idea of my background, but I had a desire to work hard, to show my loyalty, and to excel in my job. I wanted to earn my spot in the real world.

Part of the pride I had as a prostitute was that I existed outside of reality. I had a fake name and worked hours that I pleased. I functioned outside of society and I used to thrive in knowing that. Here I was, starting at eight and finishing at five, working in society, right in the middle of the city, wearing a uniform that was unbecoming, and working for the minimum wage. Not only that but I was unpopular; no one idolized me at all. A few of the girls gathered together for cigarettes throughout the day. Meanwhile I was left doing the dishes or running the rubbish out.

I took my Bible to work every day and read it on my lunchbreak. I struggled with the music at times because it reminded me of my past, the porn and the life in the parlour. Most songs on the radio had become perverted in my mind because of the memories attached. I made a conscious effort to not sing along with them because I knew I was still so vulnerable to temptations. I took my Bible and read it every day during my breaks, because that anchored me in my spirit back to the truth that was setting me free. I was used to not caring about what people thought, especially as a prostitute, so I didn't care about the glances and murmurs from my workmates.

They would question me but with mockery in their tone, and soon I realized I was being given the dirty jobs and being scoffed at behind my back. It used to irritate me that these girls thought they were so tough and found it fun to be cruel to me, the girl who read her Bible at lunch time, yet had no idea of where I'd come from. I was desperate to fight off that irritation though, as I knew my identity couldn't be in who I used to be; they couldn't know me as that. They had to know me as Marie, a Christian; free, joyful and someone who loved them.

I'd pray for them and I'd let them know. I asked them if they wanted me to pray for them. They didn't seem to mind and within a few months they could tell I was being authentic.

Despite the mockery I still had joy in me though, joy that I had received that just couldn't leave. Even though it was hard work for not much money, I was still full of this joy.

I saved my money every week and broke each bill up into minimum repayments. By the end of the week I'd be left with ten dollars, sometimes less to buy my lunch. I didn't mind. I was being looked after by God in other ways.

I think the most transforming part of walking this out was doing it humbly. I was not liked, I was earning hardly anything, and I was putting into practice the word of God each day. It was, without a doubt, the Spirit of God who enabled me to read and follow the Bible; to think of others better than myself, and to not worry about what I will eat or drink or what I'd wear, because God takes care of me.

The Bible says also to turn the other cheek, and when someone curses you, to bless them. Love is the greatest goal; as Christ loved me and forgave me, so should I forgive others. What could possibly happen to change the inside of a prostitute, with a mind that was selfish, blind and filthy, into someone who thinks of others and wants to build a free and clean life? Jesus Christ. He's real.

Philippians 1.6 says that he promises to complete the good work he started in me. Psalm 23.3 says, *"He restores my soul."* Jesus Christ can and will restore your soul. You will be so full of joy, because knowing him is the highest purpose of life that you'll ever receive.

Jesus was committed to my healing; he didn't automatically take away my debts, but I was always looked after.

I needed new clothes, but I didn't even think to worry about it. I had only one or two outfits in my wardrobe. One day I was at my brother's place and they had just been given several bags of clothes from some good friends, who didn't fit them anymore. I tried them on and, to my surprise, they were the perfect fit. I couldn't believe it! Suddenly I had a wardrobe full of clothes and shoes.

Often my boss would let us take muffins home at the end of the day, so not only did I get a free lunch but my family also benefitted.

I prayed for a miracle, that my bills would be wiped away, but I knew God was teaching me to be responsible, something I had never been, and to face them and not run away. I had to be diligent. Every week I'd pay a little bit off each bill and most weeks I had maybe five or ten dollars left over for myself.

I wasn't materialistic at all; as far as I was concerned I was the richest I had ever been. I had no addictions, I had a roof over my head, and I had the peace and joy that I had searched everywhere for but had never found until Jesus was the king of my life.

God has always provided for me in my life with him. I have never needed food, clothing or shelter. He has always looked after me.

These are just the physical ways God has been with me and helped me to leave the world of prostitution and meth. The spiritual change was way more profound than anything else though. Jesus Christ could see I was in pain, hurting and broken. I was probably close to killing myself in one way or another. He then stepped in. He said he would give me his life, filled with joy and peace, his inheritance in heaven, his salvation, his blood that has the power to cleanse my sin, and in exchange he would take my pain, my sadness, and all my sin. I just had to simply believe.

It was like he was leaning down from Heaven with his hand outstretched saying "Do you trust me?" Once I looked away from my mess and towards him, I trusted him, I believed his word, and all of a sudden I was transferred from the kingdom of utter pain and darkness into his kingdom of light. He rescued me from the grave, he filled my life with light, he turned my sadness into pure joy, he led me to a place where I can eat and sleep in safety and no one makes me afraid, and his perfect love has cast out ALL my fear.

22

King's Table

A month or so after moving to the South Island, I was in my room and had tempting thoughts harassing my mind. I had prayed, I'd spoken out the Bible and the promises of healing and deliverance, but I still felt somewhat overcome. I went to sleep exhausted, and that night I had my first proper dream with Jesus Christ in it. The dream started off with me as a prostitute, walking down the main street of Auckland; it was a total re-enactment of the time, just a few months earlier, when I had been walking down the main street of Auckland and I'd run into the street evangelist. In my dream, a very good-looking man came up to me. He was good looking inside and outside; I just knew he was good. He motioned for me to come home with him. I felt incredibly awed that he wanted me to come with him. I obeyed and got into the backseat of the car. He was in the front passenger seat; I couldn't see the driver. We drove to his house.

Inside it was very well lit, it was roomy and new. I saw a girl I recognised from working at a strip club with me walk across the room, holding white linen. I looked over at the good man who had brought me here. I began to take my clothes off, starting a slow dance as if I was expected to perform. To my surprise he shook his head.

"No." He waved his hands at me and then pulled out a cloth made of sacking. He put it on me, covering my outfit with his sackcloth. I wasn't overly alarmed. Usually if you are at a client's house you do what they want, and some men just want to have dinner with you... maybe that was the gig?

He handed me a bowl of porridge, then motioned me to sit down and eat it. "Eat, and get ready... because soon you'll be sitting at the king's table."

I was stunned! The king's table? I looked over and the man had disappeared. I motioned for the girl I'd recognised carrying the linen. She was obviously working here too, but what was going on?

"Where are we?" I asked.

"Don't you know? This is Jesus's house. You belong to him now. He's paid for you with the highest price," she said. It was like a flood of light hit me so hard and I woke up from the dream.

As I lay in my bed, the profound impact of the dream flooded through me and I felt the final pieces of temptation fall off me. That was the moment when I truly knew I had been transferred from the kingdom of darkness into the kingdom of light. I was truly free. It was so deeply healing in my natural world, to know that I had been purchased and now belonged to almighty God himself in the spiritual world.

It wasn't until a few weeks later that I discovered in my Bible that some scriptures specifically use the words, '*You were bought at a high price*' (1 Corinthians 7.23) and the invitation to come to the kings table, in Luke Chapter 14. The moment I read that I leapt with joy and laughed loudly. I couldn't believe it! It truly was confirmation that the dream was sent from Jesus Christ himself, to establish the truth in my heart of his ownership. I belonged to him now!

I never, ever could have possibly imagined being free, or having true peace, or being so still and content. It was like a river of peace flowing in my spirit. I'd had so many days and nights, hour upon hour of struggle, paranoia, darkness and pain, all in the midst of the glamour and lights of the sex industry.

I used to hope that one day I would be owned. One day, maybe, a man would hire me out, decide he loved me and would keep me as his own, of course with all the meth in the world at my fingertips. However, believing in Jesus Christ, I was now adopted into God's family. It sounds like a cliché sentence, but the hole in my soul was now eternally plugged up and sealed shut. There was no longer an ache but instead a deep sense of belonging. My identity was growing back, my true identity as Marie. Owned by God, provided for, loved, freed! Thank you, Jesus, for paying that high price for me to have this!

I was going to church now, dressed in the new clothes the Lord had provided. I still had my bills, and they were increasing too, but I could see God's hand. He was being a good father to me and helping me to pay them off each week. When I saw the cross on the church wall I couldn't help but sparkle inside; that cross was what had set me free. That cross meant not only I was forgiven for being the way I was, I was finally free from addiction, I was totally healed of pain and it was as though not a single hair on my head was singed in the fire I had just experienced. How great is my God? I wanted to sing of his praises so loud and for so long!

I got so excited about who Jesus was, but I found the reaction of some Christians really heart-breaking. It was as though I had just discovered the most glorious tasting bread, yet they were bored with it and had been leaving the bread aside; still having it in their house, but it had gone stale to them. I couldn't fathom that they weren't as excited about what the cross meant. Medications, police, doctors or even psychiatrists had tried to fix me from being self-destructive, addicted, suicidal and promiscuous, yet the cross of Jesus Christ had totally set me free. I didn't have too many friends because of this. I made a few close friends in the church, but they were elderly women in their sixties and seventies. I loved these women. I began going to their homes for cups of tea and was delighted to see they still had joy and hunger for God. They didn't seem to be caught up in the world of Facebook or fashion or the cares of the world. They just liked being with Jesus. The closer I got to God, the more my loneliness left me.

I shifted with my parents into a beautiful home, but I preferred to spend time in my room singing or reading the Bible, talking with God, writing and praying for people. This way of life began to really establish in me a firm foundation of life in God, with his Spirit guiding me. I was always filled with joy and peace and it would come out naturally in my job. People still had no idea I had been a prostitute living on the streets, on meth, just months earlier. I felt I didn't want my identity to become that. I really was a new creation; I was Marie.

I loved God and he loved me, so I lived that life and rarely even spoke about my past. I was devoted to getting to know God and Jesus, and learning about the Spirit who was now my helper. I prayed often, driving in my car, walking, resting; I just talked to God and included him in everything I did. The Bible says to acknowledge God in all your ways and he will direct your path, but I found it wasn't a command I had to strive to do; it was a natural part of my relationship with God. Now that his spirit lived in me I naturally flowed in conversation with him. I didn't hide anything from him either; if I had a dream about my past or a thought, I would tell him about it and he directed my path from there. He reminded me that I was loved, a new creation, free, pure, holy and blameless.

He showed me the way in life; how to be patient, kind and caring, how to love others like he had loved me. How did he do this? I would talk to him and then open the Bible and the words spoke directly to my heart and instructed me on which way to go or what to do.

Some people say I went from one addiction to another, being addicted to God.

I think I was originally designed to be addicted to God, and any other addiction is counterfeit. We were created as *'the apple of his eye,'* according to Deuteronomy 32.10. We were created to know God and be known by him; to be in relationship with him. We were born and designed to love and to worship. Worshipping God is our purpose, but many people reject God and worship other gods: drugs, success, people, alcohol, sex, shopping, eating or exercising. We all devote our lives to something; anything. It is in all of us because we were originally designed to worship God, to be loved and accepted by God, and to know him.

23

Wearing Shoes of Peace

Walking home from the coffee shop with loads of leftover muffins one day, I saw a couple of guys in the park who appeared to be homeless. It was raining and cold, and I suddenly just broke inside, remembering how hollow and lonely that existence truly was. Here I was, blessed with food, coming home from a job, safe and well, yet just months earlier I had been one of those ones in the rain with no family to go home to. I quickly rushed over and gave them the muffins and prayed with them. I shared what God had done for me. I got the feeling they weren't so interested in prayer as much as they were interested in a young girl in the park in the early evening. I felt God prompt me to go home and not to stay.

I cried for them on the way home, knowing how good my heavenly father is, how he has arms open wide, how he'd given me a Bible to build my life on, healing, provision, freedom, and most of all, adoption into his family. I was overcome with how good and kind God was to me; how just months earlier that was me alone and homeless out in the cold.

Thanking God for this, I prayed about my having a heart for the lost. Within the week I heard about a church that feeds the homeless and runs a weekly Bible study group. I was overwhelmed with excitement, that a church was helping feed the poor without judgement, helping teach them the word of God and praying for the sick. I immediately joined the group. That church became my second family, and the street men and women also became like family.

Over next two years I learned how to play again. I'd ride my bike, go to the gym with my sister, eat out with friends, laugh with family, tease my older brother, walk on the beach watching joy on children's faces, play cards with my niece or feed the ducks with her. All of those natural experiences were healing something deep in my heart.

Of course, I'd get memories still, I'd see hotels or brothels or even night clubs while out and about, and I'd have memories of the years I spent there; some of them really appealing memories of the good times. I wouldn't let any temptation take a grip on my heart though. I knew the Bible scriptures were like a sword for me. I'd just speak them to myself, hearing the truth of the Bible and feeling that peace remain, and kick out any temptation. I'd thank God for what he's rescued me from. I used the temptation of my past as a platform to thank God for what he was doing.

I really enjoyed getting to know God. I started every day with coffee in bed and chats. I sensed his presence very strongly, his peace, and his voice through the Bible. I was able to rebuild my life slowly but surely, and I had fun doing it. I know now that if he could do that for me, he could do that for any woman in the brothels.

I've thought a lot about the girls I'd known over the years. The pain I saw then really hurt my heart now as I thought back on it. At the time we were all in pain, but it was like common ground and no-one cared too much. We just lived this life that was outside of society, a camaraderie and unspoken love bonded us together. It was not a shock to us to hear of each other's abuse or weird clients; it was all part of the day to day. The highs we shared, the money, the laughs, the chats in our dressing room, sharing cigarettes, drugs, watching TV until you'd hear the chime of the bell indicating a client had arrived. The scramble together to get ready and pull your high heels back on before parading out to the client, hoping he'd pick one of us, or sometimes hoping he wouldn't pick one of us. I was close with the girls and had them on my heart now that I was living this new, peaceful existence in God's kingdom.

I truly felt like I had been adopted and placed in a completely different world; a world of love, peace, joy, provision, safety, and true healing. I felt totally washed and pure, and fully restored. I didn't see any counsellors or take any medication. Knowing Jesus Christ was enough. He restored me physically, emotionally and mentally. I was truly a new creation. If he can do that for me, he can do that for any girl working in the sex industry; a complete restoration, a total inner transformation. The Bible promises God will rescue you from the grave and flood your life with light, and that is truly what happens. Just call on the name of Jesus, repent by turning to him and giving up your life, trusting him to lead you out, and you'll never look back.

He truly does flood your life with light. I had to repent though, to turn my back on that life and cleanse and renew my mind by thinking on what he was showing me in the Bible and believing him. By not dwelling on my past or sitting there filling up my head with garbage from the TV, or music that would trigger memories. I had to change, but I could only do it with the help of Jesus; by praying to him, believing his word and feeling the power within me of his Spirit. He helped me to overcome temptation, to become patient, kind, caring, to have self-control, to forgive people and to trust him when I felt worthless. It really is a walk of faith, but the most beautiful experience!

It took me just a year and a half to completely clear my debt. I cleared the last few grand by selling my car, and my brother bought me a bike to roll around on. I worked in the café for about a year before moving on to a short stint at a supermarket.

Two years had passed now, and I was beginning to wonder if I could do a job outside of hospitality. The problem was that my record and past would surely hinder any chance of getting a proper professional job.

A couple of months after I came to the South Island, I took on a volunteer job at the hospice, a place for people in their last stages of life. Something about their need, the raw beauty of their final goodbyes and the final consolidation of their lives drew me to help them. I spent a couple of hours, once a fortnight, pushing around a drinks trolley and serving them dinner. I'd chat with them and pray, and share my faith whenever I could.

A few months after starting, however, I was called into the main office. I knew something was wrong, I could feel it in my gut. I fully believed though, that it was the sharing of my faith. It wasn't encouraged, that's for sure. However, the lady pulled out a piece of paper. "Your record has just come back, Marie. I'm sorry but we have to let you go," she said.

I understood immediately; I was being fired. That was devastating but I completely understood. I would miss that job. I felt really close with some of the patients, even though it was usually just for a brief moment. I enjoyed working alongside them and praying for them.

The timing was actually a good thing though, because I was working full time and I had started serving at the church with the street people; I was running out of steam!

Despite having had this experience more than a year earlier, I decided to go for it and apply for a job where I could help people as a support worker. I had worked in hospitality and loved it. I had been faithful, and had always had employers who looked after me.

One day I decided to apply to an advertisement for a support worker. I went to the interview feeling relaxed and confident. I had prayed before I went, and knew I could trust God to give me the job if it was right for me.

The questions seemed to be tailored around the workings of the job. I loved helping people and I was prepared to learn the ins and outs. However, as they came to the end they said if I had anything to ask or add, now was the time. They seemed glowing towards my responses and I knew I was about to drop bombshell for them!

"Yes; I've got a criminal record. I was a meth user for a couple of years and got really caught up in that world. I've been clean for two years now, and I use that bad experience as a learning curve and a tool to help others," I said.

They seemed genuinely surprised. They thanked me for my time and I left.

I felt a small, sinking feeling in my gut; I had tried, but maybe this was what God had for me; that hospitality was where I was meant to be. I was grateful for hospitality and I made up my mind that no matter what the outcome I would thank God and trust him.

A couple of weeks later I got a call to say I had been accepted and could start soon, provided I get a doctor's report to verify my sobriety and a psychiatrist report to say I was fully sane and fit for work. Hooray!

I was so excited: it was like a breakthrough into a new level for me. Thank you God! What's more, the money was almost double that in hospitality.

I was now debt free and in a job where I was helping others, and also had more money. I was in a place of my life where money was no longer a temptation but a tool to help others. The promise in Deuteronomy about God making me the head and not the tail, where instead of borrowing money I would now be the lender, was coming to pass. He is faithful and his promises prove true.

24

Real Life

I began the support work job. I worked alongside troubled teenagers for the first year. I found it really stressful and challenging, but part of me really loved it.

I was in a small team who looked after young teenagers, one at a time, as they came out of the youth justice prison. I felt sorry for them because they couldn't live in their own families, and they had too many complex behaviours to be in foster care.

I got on really well with my workmates and we often shared lots of laughs during the challenging times. We became very close. I couldn't believe I was in a role where I was actually helping people.

Working with the troubled teens was more than difficult at times. The hours were really long and I began going home too tired to pray. A few times at work situations escalated. I got punched in the face twice. Another time I was strangled against a wall. Even though I was now a Christian, it brought back traumatic feelings from my past. Most of my workmates took a couple of days off if this happened and returned to work as normal but each time it happened to me something broke inside. I had just had a whole year of living in God's presence, in safety, with peace, and now I was being abused and getting incredibly tired.

One day, I was sent home early because while driving a girl to school she began attacking me from the backseat. I got out of the car and had a full-blown panic attack. I didn't know where I was or what to do and I disconnected inside from reality. Within an hour I found myself at the dairy buying cigarettes. I was traumatized and went home and cried and cried, smoking my cigarettes.

"God you have to help me," I prayed, but darkness continued to grow inside of me like a black fog.

I stayed home for a couple of weeks crying and smoking cigarettes. I felt I'd let God down by the way I responded. How come my workmates handled situations like this and I didn't? I stopped sleeping and the perfect mental health God had given me was now cracking.

I was reluctant to go back to work but when I did my managers put me into a different section of the company and I began working alongside young autistic women in a home. I came alive in this role. I stopped smoking and slowly began to heal from the trauma of my previous role.

There were five young ladies in one house. They all had unique personalities and unique challenges but they had one thing in common; they loved each other. They were like a beautiful flatting family and the staff were amazing. We talked and had coffees on multiple occasions, sharing our stories about the fun things the girls got up to.

Every Saturday night, on my shift, I would make it fun by creating games, night-time car rides with the music blasting, or invite all their friends over for a party.

The company I worked for were incredible. I became very good friends with two people in particular, who came to help me through some more difficult times.

I worked lots and was now spending less time with God. I also began drinking wine with friends and had begun to fall in and out of the diet culture. I was still helping out at the church group and still in relationship with God but the initial zeal had gone.

I was in a challenging job and it was slowly changing me. I would have weeks when I was really good in life; loving my job and loving my faith and my family. But then I'd have days where I'd randomly get drunk or over-exercise again. I knew that cracks were beginning to appear, but I felt I had control. God was still good and he would still help me.

There was a small part of me that was curious about having a relationship. Life had been going so well; just maybe I could end up married one day! With a little encouragement from my friends I started checking out dating websites. On the very first dating site I signed up for there was a very attractive man with a glowing profile and similar interests, just staring me right in the face. I was excited and quickly sent him a message. We chatted for a few days before arranging to meet at a food fair on the other side of town.

Dating is fun, it's exciting, you don't know who there'll be; if they're the future love of your life, or if they're not going to turn up and you're left to eat ice-cream on your own, watching all the families walk by as you wait.

I remember thinking on our first meeting that if he didn't turn up that's exactly what I'd do; I always loved an excuse to eat ice-cream. He was late! But when he arrived he rushed up with a huge smile and sparkling eyes, apologizing that he had to clean the church. How could I judge him for cleaning a church?

We talked and ate kebabs and I eventually got my ice-cream. He was really fascinating; he was slightly awkward and shy and was definitely the nerdy type. He was smart, really into business and making money. I was into helping homeless people and working with adorable but hyperactive autistic girls. We had two things in common though; we both loved God and wanted to help people. Over the next week we were like excited kids, texting each other every hour or so to say funny things or chat about life and our love for people and God. We met for a second date. He wanted to have lunch at the center of the city. I thought it was going to be at a restaurant but nope, he suggested a 'bring your own' sandwich.

It was kind of romantic, but my expectations of dating were a little too high; I thought he would wine and dine me. He was still interesting though. He was a lot smarter than me and a bit older. He had his finger in lots of pies that I'd never even touched, but we got along really well.

Over the next couple of months we saw each other nearly every day. He'd pick me up in his truck and we'd have home-made dinner by the water or in a park. We would go for walks and chat for hours. He appeared to be intensely interested in me.

We began talking about the future; there was no pressure, it was just a fun conversation, exploring ideas. What would it be like if we were married? What is your dream honeymoon? He would always bring me gifts of fruit or flowers, and displayed the most genuine, gentlemanly heart I had ever seen.

I told him about my past experiences, and I decided to give him a copy of a book I had started writing about my life. He responded well, strong and calm about the fact he was dating an ex-prostitute. He appeared to be okay about it all, so I didn't need to elaborate or go into details. He read the book so there was nothing more to say. We had quickly fallen in love.

Meanwhile, life had become incredibly busy. I was renting a small apartment of my own in town, I worked four days a week at the young ladies house and I had just started leading a homeless group at the church every Monday night. I would help serve dinner, pray for people who were injured or sick, or I would help out with the Bible studies. I had become best friends with the other leaders there.

When the Bible study leaders moved to America they asked if I would step up and take over. I was really honoured and excited. I believed that God could help any person in any situation. I believed that the Bible was a tool for how to do life and also God's communication to us. Maybe this was just what I needed to help my life also? Maybe it would seal the cracks back up again.

I began studying on my days off and after work, filling my time up with Bible studies and putting together presentations for the Monday night. At times my life was so busy I felt like I could hardly breathe. My roots were deep in God because of the first year of my faith and how full-on it had been. I still maintained my morning coffee date with him, reading the Bible and chatting away, often praying for help during the day or celebrating life's fun times with thankfulness to God. I started to feel distant though; the cracks were still there.

25

Quakes in the Soul

There was a shooting in Christchurch and a few of us from my company went down to relieve the Christchurch staff, who needed time off. It had been a terror attack in the city. I went down there feeling quite secure in who I was, and stable as a person. During this time, I formed a really strong bond with a guy called Dave who I worked with. He had a similar past to mine, and I opened up a lot about my addiction years.

Being in Christchurch was eerie; the atmosphere was pure fear, because of what had just happened. Dave and I made light of it by trying to have a good time outside our working hours, talking and laughing about our crazy drug years. It brought in a lot of temptation for me from my past. I usually avoided the topic of drugs for this very reason but my bond with Dave was strong, and I depended on his friendship during our time in Christchurch.

We worked crazy hours so I had no time to pray, and the atmosphere was traumatising. I just couldn't pick up my Bible. Within days I stopped sleeping.

In Christchurch, surrounded by fear and without any sleep, I lost touch with God and my faith. I became lost inside and questioned everything I believed in.

We returned home and it took me a couple of weeks to find my bearings again, to sense God's presence and read my Bible. I continued to work long hours, but was becoming more and more exhausted. I would still struggle to not get drunk when I was having wine with friends. Even my Christian friends drank a glass of wine, so I assumed it was okay.

I managed to gain some distance between Dave and myself and fought hard to deny our attraction to each other. We had bonded during a traumatic time in Christchurch. We had visited the shooting site where the blood was still fresh, and we had talked with people who had been close by and seen it. We distracted ourselves by talking about drugs and sex, and I was so tired that my brain disconnected momentarily, and I wasn't sure if I was in reality or not.

I knew I had to slow down, but I couldn't. I taught the Bible every Monday night, went to work four days a week, was building an intense romantic relationship with my boyfriend and was also attempting to go jogging every day at 5am.

When I first became a Christian and got out of the meth world, I would spend hours and days lying on my bed just resting, praying, being thankful and healing. Here I was, three years later, burning the candle at both ends, but because it was for good things, I didn't see a problem. I was finally living the dream of helping people, but during this time of helping people, it had reopened old traumas and the cracks had formed.

Helping people can be messy work; you get yelled at, let down and taken for granted. I still did it though, because there were a few shining stars amongst all the people I was helping. They made it all worth it.

One night, I had a horrible nightmare. In the dream, I was being chased by three demonic, gigantic beasts and on top of them was a demon driving them towards me. It was awful. That whole day, I felt completely jaded at work and unable to concentrate. I felt there was something off in the spirit realm around my life. I couldn't figure it out.

That evening, my boyfriend picked me up in his truck and we drove down to the marina with our thermos of soup. He appeared quieter than usual; he wasn't his usual chatty self. I asked him how he was. How did the evening at his parents' house go? He was quiet again, but then slowly admitted that his parents, who I'd met only once, did not approve of our relationship. I was surprised because I assumed I had made a good impression. He'd told them a little bit about my past, and they'd become really concerned, and warned him I was not the right girl for him.

"But I've changed now. The Bible says if you're born again, you're a new person. Don't they share the same beliefs?" I asked.

He shook his head; they were Christians but obviously didn't share that belief about me. I was used goods.

"Well, what do you think?" I asked.

He looked at me with sadness in his eyes, and completely out of the blue he told me, "I have to honour my parents."

I remember the shock coming over me like a cold blanket. I became numb. I had been jaded all day because of my nightmare, I was overly exhausted from my life commitments, and now the love of my life was breaking up with me so suddenly. I disconnected right then and there.

All of a sudden, Marie disappeared deep down inside of me. I couldn't reach her. I felt God was in another room, and this fractured part of my self emerged, completely jaded and shocked.

"Take me home," I said.

He started the truck, and we headed off through the city towards my apartment. How can this be true? We had driven this same route night after night, totally in love. There had been no warning. I felt like I was falling; my good, stable God-loving self was falling. I felt empty. I hated how he still walked me to my door; I couldn't understand that.

Once inside, I began to sob. I was, all of a sudden, in physical pain. My body reacted, and I had immediate diarrhoea. I rushed to the bathroom just in time and sat there crying for ages. Something had broken inside of me. The cracks that had been forming over the last year had suddenly broken my soul like one massive earthquake.

26

Splitting

I cried all night long. I was unable to go to bed because I dreaded waking up and having to face the breakup all over again.

The next day I struggled to go to work. I was still so disconnected, yet I had to do this big life I had created. I had to work with these young women who relied on me, I had to do my study for outreach; I had to live when I felt like I had died!

I cried most of the day at work and was sent home early because I couldn't concentrate. I felt terrible, knowing I had just put their lives at risk by driving around distracted and crying half the day. I was fortunate that my co-worker was there for some of the day and took over for me.

The only person in the world I could bear hanging out with was Dave. During our time in Christchurch, he had become a really good friend. He was my age. He had experienced a really crap deal in life, but he had such a positive attitude and loved his work helping people. He was completely rough around the edges. He smoked, drank like a fish and got stoned on his days off. He was a good friend though; we got on really well.

I rang him and told him about the breakup and we met for a drink and to talk. I talked and talked, and as I talked I drank. He didn't think anything of it and drank with me. I got so drunk, and then stumbled home.

Inside my apartment I cried and cried again. Not only had I broken up with my boyfriend, but I felt completely broken inside. I didn't want to talk to God. I felt as though he still cared and still loved me, but he was in a different room and there was huge walls of pain separating me from him.

Over the next couple of weeks I stopped going into work, I stopped my morning runs and I stopped my Bible study. I just couldn't do life at all. I hardly showered, I ate unhealthy, easy fast-food, and I didn't care. I started smoking, I bought wine every night and I drank, either at the pub with Dave or alone in my apartment listening to music that was either angry, lost or sad.

I knew I had fallen, I had slipped, but the scary thing was I couldn't stop myself. Usually, if I'd drink a few wines over the past couple of years, I would correct myself quickly and moderate it better. I would still talk to God through it all, and he would always help me overcome my challenges as a new Christian. But this time was different. I was in a big black hole; something inside of me had broken.

One day, a workmate of mine had noticed I hadn't been going to work much, and had been at the pub a lot with Dave. She told me it was better for me to smoke pot than it was to drink alcohol. "You'll be less depressed," she suggested.

Oh my goodness! If she had only known who she was talking to! I was drinking and smoking so much that, in my fragile state of mind, I decided that was a very logical idea. Maybe I could even get in touch with God again if I was drinking less? Maybe I'd put on less weight? Maybe I'd finally be able to sleep and go back to work. I knew it was wrong, but it also seemed very right. I agreed and began buying pot. The drinking, however, didn't stop.

My family were concerned, which I absolutely hated. How could I tell them I was struggling like this? They'd be mortified and heartbroken. I kept up appearances by visiting every couple of weeks or texting. Dave, however, had quickly become my new best friend.

My emotions had taken a sudden crash. I was no longer positive and full of energy. Now I lay in my bed listening to sad music and crying about the brokenness of me, completely unaware that I was adding to the pieces of my life falling to the floor. Pain had gripped me hard, and it was dragging me back to my old life.

Dave and I became even closer during this time. He made me laugh. We talked for hours, sometimes, about life; its craziness, drugs and sex. He had a past similar to mine and so we connected on that level quite a lot. We spent a lot of our time partying together and one night I invited him back to my place. We started seeing each other more frequently, texting, drinking, partying and sleeping together. It all happened so fast. I really liked who he was, how funny he was and his outlook on life. He was so fun to be around and I felt like I could be myself with him. The only thing wrong was there was a huge part of myself that was broken and not talking to God.

I had limited my contact with my Christian friends because I was so ashamed of how far I had fallen. When I was with Dave I felt the only sense of relief and happiness possible for me during that time. I was so reluctant, though, to connect with him as a permanent boyfriend. He wasn't a Christian, and even though I was far away from God, our beliefs were so different. I still believed in God and I still knew he loved me. I also knew one day I'd find my footing again and be okay.

Things inside me began to get darker and darker. I moved in with some Christian friends who I had previously been very close to. They knew I was going through a rough time and was partying quite a bit, but they loved me anyway. They had rules about drugs in the house and encouraged me to get back in touch with God and find my faith again. I felt like a switch had gone off inside of me though; all my old evil parts were rushing through me, and there was almost no way to turn it off. My emotional state began to deteriorate quickly.

In the mornings I would feel hyper, I would think of crazy ideas and come up with different plans every day. It was during these times of hyper-ness I would lose all sense of judgement. Then, in the afternoons I would often crash, climb back into bed and get completely stoned and cry as blackness tormented my soul. This was scary but I thought this was just reality. I continued to drink at night, often alone in my room listening to music, and I would spend the day getting stoned.

27

The Trapdoor

One day I was lying on my bed thinking of how much I had given myself away; to drugs, to Dave, and to alcohol. I felt like it was just one door after another being opened back to the monster of my past. I felt like I was slipping down a very familiar slope.

The idea that came to me one day excited me. It gave me a sense of power and control, as I knew that once I made that choice, I would let everything go. I'm already having sex so why not get paid for it?

When I began to think like that, I felt as though a whole new personality entered into my body! My eyes lit up with excitement but I shook with fear at the same time. However something clicked inside of me and in my reality, returning to sex work was the perfect answer. It may help me take control back in my life.

This was the exact, same pattern repeating in my life. Whenever I experienced trauma, I would retreat to what I knew; drugs, sex and money. Somehow, I always thought that it would solve all my problems. I registered again with the agency and I booked my hotel. I felt as though I was about to take a giant leap off the diving board. I told my flatmates that I was going out. I made appointments for daytime only.

I drove into town on that first morning, shaking with fear. "Marie! What are you doing?" I felt an incredible urge to pull over. I had a family who loved me! What would they think? I wanted to stop the car and go home, but the day before, when the wild idea had come to me, a very silent, dominant part of myself resurrected from the dead and was slowly taking over. I had absolutely no connection, the day before, to the slightest care about my family.

My hands shook as I entered the hotel; what if I get caught by someone I know? What if I get killed? I had no idea how or why I continued to go through with it. It was a crazy idea at the time, and now I was committed.

Prostitution is like poisonous candy. It looks so good on the outside, and that's what drew me back in. I would have a different name, I would be sober, I would claim back control of my life. I wouldn't ever have to worry about money, and I would be wanted. This is what happened in the first couple of weeks.

I felt free in a way because I had let down my defences and embraced the career path that I had spent years avoiding. I kept my own promise and only selected certain people, assuming I could keep safe this way. It was the candy part, the star-studded curtain I had entered into again. I was popular, I made a lot of money, things seemed to be going well, but my heart still fluttered with fear at every new knock on the door.

Dave wasn't happy about my decision. He told me he would make sure I was safe, but he didn't agree with what I was doing. I told him I was having fun and I could keep safe. I created a whole new persona under a new name.

I stood in my bedroom at home one morning, looking in my wardrobe. I fingered through all the clothes that Marie wore. I looked at the hoodies, the dresses, the jeans, the shoes and the collection of funky tights I had collected over the years. I didn't know what to wear, I couldn't pick an outfit because I couldn't identify with Marie anymore. In just two weeks my new persona had consumed me.

What scared me was how I felt out of control, sometimes. One morning I'd feel so alive and filled with ideas about sex and drugs and life, with no fear or sense of right and wrong. Then, at night, I'd be crying and drinking, wishing I was dead, but somehow I couldn't find the courage to die.

I found middle ground sometimes but this was when I reasoned with myself that prostitution was helping my life; I was getting stoned less, I felt loved, even though I knew my clients went home to their own families and lives at the end of the day.

The persona took over so much that my flatmates started picking it up and questioning me about where I was going during the day. One thing about me is that I can't lie. I'm terrible at lying, especially to friends, so I told them. I promised them I was safe, and no one knew where we lived.

This candy was sweet, it was good. I thought, just maybe I had avoided the poison. I began to get cocky about my work and started extending my hours to nights.

One day a client came in and pulled out a bag of meth. As soon as I saw it I wanted it. Meth was just part of the game and was surely about to happen. Part of me wondered if half the reason I entered into sex work was to find meth again. I had thought about it, but it was one tiger I intentionally didn't actively try and wake up. But if it was to find me, that was another story.

Here it was, being offered to me in large amounts by a seemingly nice guy. I buckled at the knees and went all in. I had opened the final door. I had relapsed.

For a moment, in this world, I felt like a free bird, living and doing whatever I wanted. This was the star-studded curtain; this was the candy.

Getting high again for the first time in three years felt absolutely liberating. I was blinded, for that small amount of time in my hotel room, that this was what it is like. Suddenly I wanted to give my life to it.

In the third week back, I continued to dabble in the meth, but it was few and far between, as this guy only visited sometimes. I began really looking forward to that time, knowing I was one step away from being a full-blown addict again.

When I was in my hotel room in this persona, I felt free, happy, and in control. It was when I went home that I felt the split happen in my mind. I would still come home and look at my Bible on the shelf, I would look at the clothes I used to wear and I would talk to my flatmates about their day and sometimes about God. They were right in front of me, yet so far away. It was like a sudden, sharp jerk from one person to the next.

I struggled to identify with Marie. As I lay in my bed at night the horror would dawn on me about what I was doing. I was addicted to sex work and I knew it. There was a rush, never knowing who would be next. There was the compliments and the money, the hotels and the independence. So, every day I would wake up and go back.

The man with the meth returned. He began disclosing about how he was in a gang. He had changed his attitude towards me. He'd become paranoid. He mentioned that I could get killed if I left town; that I could shortly be owned.

The candy suddenly became sour. I stumbled through the star-studded curtain. I handed him back the meth pipe. "I've had enough," I said. He looked me straight in the eyes for a moment; it was long enough to send shivers through my entire body.

I remembered now. I remembered what ownership was like. I remembered that gangs existed. What was worse, meth yoked you to them, and as a woman working on my own, I was suddenly in a very vulnerable position.

After he left, my bubble had completely burst. I had waves of terror rolling over me. It was late; close to midnight. What if he was waiting for me by my car? What if he came back with his gang? He had appeared really nice and trusting, but had turned into the devil himself!

I frantically packed up my bag, grabbed my wine from the fridge, rolled a cigarette with shaking hands and fled the hotel. I'd became paranoid in a split second. What if he was following me? All of a sudden I didn't want to do this anymore. The fear came flooding back. I got in my car and began to drive, but I didn't want to drive home in case he followed me.

What had I done? I could feel Marie coming back inside me again, taking control and directing me to my brother's house. I had to tell him what I'd done. I had to get help. The bubble had burst, and I was no longer in the candy store.

My brother opened his door and scratched his head. "Marie, it's one in the morning! What's going on?"

I walked in and sat on his couch and buried my face in my hands. My heart was pounding. "I've done something," I said.

He scoffed a bit and shook his head. "Come on, Marie. What's this all about? I know you're sad about your breakup. Surely it can't be that bad," he said.

I froze in my seat. I had to tell him, but how? "I think I'm in trouble," I cried.

"What do you mean?" His voice began to raise.

"I smoked meth again and I relapsed and went back to prostitution!"

"What?" I glanced up to see the colour drain from his face. "What did you do, Marie?" he yelled.

"I'm in trouble," I sobbed.

My brother exploded! "Who do I have to fuckin' pay? What have you done? Do I have to go and smash someone's face in? What have you done?" he was screaming.

I could hear his wife making slow movements in the background. It was 1 a.m. and his whole family were asleep in their beds.

"I'm sorry," I sobbed. "I thought it was safe. I thought would be fun. I don't know what came over me! I thought I could go back, but it's just as bad, and I'm sorry and I need to quit! I'm so sorry!"

I begged him to understand and help me, but his rage began to explode onto the floor in front of me. He was so mad I thought he was going to hit me.

There was at least half an hour of him yelling and my crying before he finally began pacing the floor with a plan.

"Fine. We are going to the bay tomorrow. You can come with us and sort out your shit. I'll help you. You can stay on my couch tonight." He went off to get me some blankets.

As I lay on his couch, high and unable to sleep, I didn't want to be a prostitute anymore. I didn't want to have drugs anymore. I wanted to change. I missed God. I forgot how scary and terrifying the world was. If I'd got owned, I would have gone through all of that trauma again.

I stayed a couple of days in a bach in the bay with my brother's family. I could hardly talk; the drugs began to drain from my body, leaving me feeling sick, unable to eat properly or hold a conversation. I was meant to be getting my shit together, but all I could focus on was getting through the next hour.

I talked briefly with my brother about it during the weekend. I promised him I'd never go back. I promised him I would get help and get back on track.

28

Train Wreck

I returned home and was left to deal with my mental state alone. I felt fractured. I'd become another person in the sex industry, for the previous few weeks. I'd been high and drunk more often than not. Here I was alone in my room with no plan and no hope. I stayed in bed and cried for a couple of days.

I felt my moods elevate again for hours at a time; I'd come up with plans to get a new job, plans to go on a health kick. But then they'd come crashing down and I'd be wrecked with anxiety, unable to breathe and terrified of life itself. I felt completely unwell in my mind. I wore hoodies and tights and spent most of my time smoking cigarettes, listening to music, crying and writing out my despair in my journal.

One day, when the cloud lifted, I applied at a café. It was my favourite café in the whole world. I began to pray to God again and decided to join in on a home-group held at my flat.

My old church friends arrived. I'd been excited to see them again, but when I did, it felt as though they were a whole world away. Did they know what I'd done? I felt shame and embarrassment so I kept things short and disappeared to my room. I couldn't deny it; the peace that was on their faces, the light in their eyes. God was real and I was very, very, far away.

I started at the café, I was so excited and grateful for the job, and determined to keep my health kick up. I worked hard, but on my bike-ride home the very same day I had been so excited and thankful for the job, something inside of me switched. Suddenly, I didn't want to go back. I didn't want anything more to do with that café.

I went out for dinner with my flatmate that night. We had pizza and played board games, and I felt my mood rising so high, out of control, and my thoughts began to race. I would become a prostitute again! I told myself that in my head and got really excited about the idea. I lost all sense of judgement again and it was like a light went on. My friend recognised I was hyper and we talked and laughed throughout the meal. Meanwhile inside, I was planning my next move.

I quit the café job by email that evening and quickly set up my escort account again. I booked a hotel and packed a bag and the next morning I was off.

I had this really scary feeling that something was wrong with me. Maybe I had two personalities. It was as though one day I was trying to get my faith back on track, eat healthy and work in a café and the next day I wanted to be a prostitute.

Work was exactly the same as always. The first week was amazing. I made lots of money, felt on top of the world, got high again, then bang. The curtain would close, the candy would become sour. A client would be a gang member, and I'd get followed in my car by motorcycles.

It all became incredibly traumatising really fast, all over again. Why did I not remember these horrible times? I would go home to my flat and sleep on my flatmate's bedroom floor and cry because I was so scared.

I wouldn't work for a couple of days after getting a scare, and I'd find myself in a state of violent anxiety and paranoia. Then I'd feel almost no will to live, and so I'd desperately come up with a plan to save my own life and go back to work safely.

I'd book hotels and keep clients to the ones I had already seen. I limited my hours, but it wasn't enough. I let my guard down one night and again, a gang member high on meth came in for a couple of hours, casing my hotel for drugs, and telling me I was owned.

Once he left I fled again, this time to Dave's house. I slept in his flat for a couple of days, absolutely petrified. Once the fear subsided my moods would cycle from low to high in the space of an hour. It scared me and I'd find myself tormented by my own mind.

Dave went to work one morning and I was too scared to stay alone in his house. I was still wasted from the night before, and tried to drive my car. I drove it into a kerb, slashing the tyre and smashing into a parked car. I pulled over and limped back to Dave's house, crying. I didn't care about the car; it was just a symbol of my wrecked life.

Life had crashed and burned again. I lived in a state of cold fear of gangs, but completely out of control of my own choices. When I felt up, I'd be really up, making crazy decisions around sex and drugs or Dave. When I was low, I was begging God to end my life. These were rapid cycles of mood; sometimes I'd experience them all in the same day. There was hardly any middle ground anymore. I needed help.

I called my friend Mandy from a church I'd gone to when I first moved to the new city. She and her husband had prayed with me when I first got out of meth, and they'd helped me build my life again. Mandy came over and picked me up. She took me back to her house, but even there I didn't feel safe. Paranoia was like a demon that possessed me. I couldn't sit still. 'What if I'd been followed? There's no end to this; the gang will get me. I'm going to die!' It was horrific.

Mandy and my old church pastors' came over and prayed for me. I still felt as though God was very far away. I couldn't see any hope. It wasn't like the first time when I prayed; there wasn't peace. I only felt fear. The pastors were so nice and non-judgemental; they even said it was an honour to help me. I felt God was far away from me, but I sensed him in their love.

Mandy rang the hospital, and took me in for an appointment. I explained how I felt like I had two personalities; one day I'd feel strong, like I wanted to be normal and sometimes that very same day I'd switch and be devoting myself to drugs and sex work. A whole new persona would come on. I explained how my moods drove me up and down; when I was in despair I was suicidal, and when I was high I was excessive in my life choices. In those choices I lost all sense of judgement and reason. I talked about how I'd lost my faith and couldn't find it again; how it all happened when I had a breakup.

The doctors admitted me to the psychiatric unit. This was a huge deal for me, but a huge relief at the same time. After all God had done for me, I ended up back in the psych unit; what a disgrace! I had fallen so far. I thought of how many times I'd shared my testimony with other believers, people on the street, in my church and in my workplaces, and here I was back in a psych ward. I was beyond humbled; I was riddled with shame.

The doctors put me on medication immediately and injected me with mood stabilizers. I felt like a numb zombie for the first couple of days. I was in shock that I was in there. I sat outside and smoked a lot. I lay on my bed in complete silence, defrosting from the fear. I ate whatever they served; my health kick was long gone. I cried a lot too.

I had to tell my family where I was and that I'd relapsed. My brother didn't reply, my sister also had to stop communicating. They were deeply hurt and had children to protect. Mum and Dad were absolutely distraught. How could I have done this to the family again? I didn't know. I felt bad and I was sorry.

The drugs they gave me at the hospital put me into a mood that was normal; I wasn't high or low, and I could think clearly. I began to really see the damage I'd done and my sense of judgement came back; I knew now it was wrong.

I woke up every day and cried and cried because I'd lost my family again. What had I done? I had completely trashed my life again. I was working in a job helping others, I was in a church helping people, God loved me and I knew that. What was wrong?

A week into my stay at the hospital, the doctors diagnosed me with bipolar disorder. It was a bit of a relief at first; I didn't have multiple personalities or schizophrenia, but I had a mental illness. Had I always had a mental illness? Where was God in all this?

Since my mood had stabilized, I'd begun to talk to God again. I prayed and cried for his help; his help to fix my family, for them to forgive me, for God to heal their broken hearts and to help me start a new life.

One day I was sitting down after lunch and a sudden urge to throw up what I had eaten came over me; I was fat now! I rushed to the bathroom and threw up my lunch. Afterwards I cried because I hadn't done this in years. Why, all of a sudden, now? I talked to my nurse and he told me it was normal to have weird behaviours come out, as ways of coping. I did this a couple of times during my stay but this also eventually dropped off.

I stayed in the hospital for a month. My body was gaining weight from the medication and the food, but I had no energy to care. I slept most of the time. When I was awake I'd either sit and smoke or lie in the silence of my room.

29

The Silent Night

When I went home to my flat, nothing had changed. I was lucky to be allowed back, after what I'd put my flatmates through. I stayed in my room most of the time, lying on my bed. I was too medicated to focus on watching TV or reading. Even listening to music was too much.

I cried because I felt completely broken. I was in this middle-ground zone with my mood, yet completely numb. I went to bed at 5:30pm every night and slept until 8 the next morning.

I couldn't live like this. I had to do something to help myself. I was still eating a lot of sugar foods, thinking this was okay. I was still smoking cigarettes and not being too bothered about it.

But one day I decided to try to heal my life again. I cut down my smoking and went out once a day for a walk. I would come home exhausted, and that would trigger an anxiety attack about how my life was so broken. I'd just start crying and not know why. I found it almost impossible to have a conversation with anyone except my parents.

One day, I heard that my ex-boyfriend's father had passed away. I contacted him and he replied, grateful to hear from me and wanting to meet up at the beach. For the first time in six weeks, something came alive in me; I was excited.

I met him at the beach, nervous about how much I'd changed, and unsure if I could explain the past few months. He seemed really happy to see me and said he was so sorry he had rejected me like that. I forgave him. Something in my heart warmed at seeing him again. We prayed together and decided to start dating again.

I went home shaking with excitement and fear. I was so unwell. How could I maintain a relationship? Yet this could be God, helping me build my life again. We decided to take things slowly.

I moved out of the country house I shared with my flatmates to one of my boyfriend's rental houses in the city. It was a breath of fresh air, with light-filled rooms and surrounded by beautiful walks. I saw my boyfriend every other day but took time to sleep, walk, eat, heal, and slowly read my Bible.

I struggled to hear from God because of my medication. My brain was still damp and foggy, yet I was calm most of the time now, and managed to read the Bible. It reminded me that God is a healer, and can restore me back to health.

My brother and sister made contact again, but it was heart-breaking to see them while feeling so disconnected from reality. I was unable to talk much; I couldn't handle more than half an hour of conversation.

After visiting my brother and sister, I went to my parents' place. I cried and cried. I felt so unwell. How come I couldn't talk anymore? Where was my personality? This was the hardest time of all. I was gaining weight and losing my personality. The only positive was I wasn't high or really low. I decided to come off my medications.

I prayed and prayed, then talked with my case manager about it. I researched about a diet that might help the brain heal itself with fruits and vegetables filled with nutrients, and I decided to take a leap of faith. As long as I stayed away from alcohol and drugs and cigarettes, I could manage my mental health. With prayer, a good diet and regular exercise, perhaps I could get the healing I needed.

I wanted to be a better girlfriend, a better sister and a better daughter. I needed to communicate better, so I decided to come off two of the medications. The first week was rough. I felt myself drop really low in my mood, where I was crying all the time again for no reason. But this time, instead of sinking into despair or clutching for drugs and alcohol, I grabbed my Bible and did what I used to do in the beginning. I read it out loud to myself, through tears, trusting that God would help me, and that he loves me. Usually a day later I'd feel the cloud lift. Slowly but surely, my moods regulated.

One day I was sitting outside having lunch with my boyfriend. He had been distant again, and keeping me away from his family events. "Are you ashamed of me?" I asked.

He lowered his head. Sadness fell over his face and he slowly nodded. I wasn't shocked. He'd done this before. His family had never liked me, and now we were back together, he hadn't told them. He was afraid of their reaction and desperate for their approval.

Suddenly, he wasn't my strong, handsome boyfriend anymore. He was weak, and I was stupid. "It's over," I said. I emotionally withdrew from him.

Instantly, he begged me to forgive him and give him another chance. He said he was sorry for being ashamed of me, and that he would change. Something in me didn't break this time, though. I didn't get re-traumatised, I didn't shatter or disconnect from God. I felt calm and stable.

I was training myself to turn to God, and my life was completely still, unlike the chaotic busyness of work that it once had been. All day, I was alone with God.

I moved out of the house that he owned, and into a house owned by a woman in my church. It too was surrounded by beautiful walks, and I had a lovely flatmate.

I was nervous when I moved in, because I was still unemployed and sleeping most of the time. I was praying more now, though, and my senses were picking up God's presence again. I could feel his peace and began having moments of joy again.

I lapsed in my diet quite a bit after the breakup, and began eating lots of sugar, indulging in blocks of chocolate and ice-cream or packets of biscuits. After each time I did this, I'd cry, and my anxiety would go through the roof.

I started linking diet, exercise and mental health. I read that binge eating was a common occurrence for people with bipolar. I had a big fear of getting fat, and I was also really poor and unable to afford it. This behaviour had to stop! I prayed and found some Bible verses that helped me gain the inner strength to quit eating sugary food. When I felt overwhelmed with a desire to eat uncontrollably, I'd compensate by going for a walk and thanking God for his strength.

I applied for a job at a retail store and got it. I was so excited; it was exactly what I needed. It was a job where I would be home in the afternoons and in bed by 7:30pm. I still had time to pray, and I wasn't getting traumatised or stressed. But could I keep up? It was a fast-paced, full-time active role, but something in me loved the idea of it. It would keep me fit and focused.

I joined a team of light-hearted, fun people who didn't take life too seriously. I had brilliant managers who encouraged me as I worked. I had come off my medication by now, believing that with a good lifestyle, I could manage my bipolar. I was working well, keeping fit and active and in bed by 7:30 each night.

Suddenly the world ground to a halt as a virus called COVID 19 spread through country after country. My job shut down for three weeks. During this time, I continued to get better, strengthening myself by keeping fit, resting well and eating a balanced diet. Once the health threat had lifted, I returned to work, but the overwhelming amount of work we had to catch up on hit me in the face. I was now running around the store picking items for online orders, and the boss was constantly in our ears about our times, and wanting updates. Pressure snowballed on me; my heart was always fearful and stressed. This was no longer an easy job. Instead, we were driven to achieve almost impossible results. I came home each day exhausted and crying from tiredness.

I decided one day to change my diet; maybe that would help me focus more at work. Around the same time, I stopped sleeping, waking up several times in the night with anxiety.

We opened the store to the public, but by this stage I had begun unravelling. My normal job routine returned, but I was becoming overwhelmed at the slightest challenge. I found myself breaking down and crying. Everything would go black around me and I'd have to take a break. It was humiliating. How am I not handling my job anymore?

I'd have several days like this, followed by a day of extreme energy. I'd feel the energy surging through me, driving me higher and higher! I'd work really fast, and I didn't need much food or sleep. After work, I'd go for a run. I felt like nothing could calm me down. It was scary and exhilarating at the same time.

One morning, as I was driving to work, a thought popped into my head. What if the gangs from last year saw me working in the retail shop and came to get me? This fear became a reality in my mind. Paranoia gripped me like ice, all over my body. I fumbled throughout the whole day, struggling to concentrate.

That day, my brother popped in to visit me during work. He could see I was making mistakes and trying not to cry. I told him about my fears and how I wasn't sure if they were real or not.

I drove home that day with the fear melting away almost as quickly as it had come. After talking to my brother, I could tell it had been false. I looked completely different now, and the gangs wouldn't care about me anymore. Why had I lived a whole day in such fear? I knew then that I was getting unwell again.

I fought it hard. I got home and watched documentaries on diet and bipolar. I then took all my groceries and threw them in the rubbish, blaming the food for making me sick. I went out and brought over a hundred dollars' worth of food that was supposedly good for helping bipolar. I felt somewhat in control again.

The next day I had a surge of energy again, this time with crazy ideas about returning to prostitution; wouldn't it be fun? Easier money? I'd probably have better self-esteem. By lunchtime my mood had crashed again. Suddenly, I felt hopeless.

My employers were incredibly supportive. I told them about my struggles with bipolar, but promised them I was fixing it. However, my mood continued to drive me like a roller coaster with no breaks. I was up and down, often daily. The diet made things worse. My sleeping became erratic again, my moods changed daily, my thoughts went from wanting to achieve a hundred different things to feeling suicidal and hopeless.

I fought the urge to go back on medication for ages; I was believing God would heal me, or I'd find the right diet to regulate my emotions. However, as these days became more erratic, I came to the point where I didn't know what would be more painful. My bipolar was now controlling my life, but the side of effects of the medication would also control my life.

One day at work, things got really bad again. I started the day confident and hoping I could finish it well, but by mid-morning I was overwhelmed at the cages of stock I had to finish. I became so overwhelmed that I couldn't remember what aisle I was in or what my next task was.

I went home early, in tears, completely embarrassed and disappointed that I couldn't even work in retail. I called the doctor and booked an appointment to go back on medication.

Things at home worsened. I stopped drinking water and I couldn't function enough to make a proper meal. I wasn't sleeping. Everything seemed black. God felt like he was in a different room, and I was isolating myself away from my friends. By the time I arrived at the doctor's, I was a crying mess, overwhelmed by the cruelness of bipolar.

In one week, I joined three different universities to study, then within a day I withdrew from them all. I had stopped eating and drinking, I was barely sleeping, and my mind changed a hundred times a day. I couldn't decide on anything, even though thoughts raced in, demanding my attention.

The doctor admitted me to the hospital.

30

Manic

I was relieved to be in hospital at first; They had taken away all the decisions from me. I would eat their meals, take the medication, and rest.

Within a couple of days, my mind slowed down, my emotions stabilised, and I felt able to relax. I'd started smoking cigarettes again, and I found myself chain smoking the days away. I made a couple of friends, but I spent most of my time lying on my bed resting.

I was assessed by several psychiatrists, and my final diagnosis was delivered. "You have reactive attachment disorder, from your childhood. I also believe you have post-traumatic stress disorder from unresolved trauma, and you have a rare bipolar disorder we rarely see here in New Zealand," he said.

I felt relieved; now I knew what was wrong, maybe we could fix it.

"Your bipolar is rapid cycling; you have despair, anxiety, mania and depression all in a day or two."

"Yes! That's what it's like. It changes so fast!" I felt finally someone understood me and could make sense of everything I was experiencing. They issued me medication and released me.

Coming home was not bliss. I unpacked my things, but suddenly I was faced with having to make a meal, to catch up on my washing, to quit smoking, and to take up my walks again. Otherwise, I would just lie in bed and get depressed. I always put a lot of pressure on myself to be a better version of myself when I start to get well, so I had taken it upon myself to do everything at once.

The medication didn't kick in straight away. I experienced my mood raging again in highs and lows. I felt as though I was back on meth; I had energy that would drive me higher and higher, and then I'd come crashing down again into blackness and despair. The most torturous part of it all was I was constantly reminding myself of how I first got well and became a Christian, how I had a sound mind and believed I was healed from fear and mood dysregulation. I still had scriptures on my wall I had made and put up when I was strong and walking with God in great faith.

I felt like a complete wreck. I was in the dark and it was all just so silent; no answers from God and no promises that I'd get better. Had I done this to myself? I was sick, unable to hold down a job, too exhausted to exercise, and I could hardly function enough to make a proper meal. This was incredibly distressing.

One day I had so much sadness in me I had a powerful fear that I would snap and return to prostitution. The thoughts came like a temptation for me; that it would be an escape. I could be someone else for a day and feel amazing. But how could I do that to my family again? I felt out of control of it, though; I was disconnecting from all reasoning.

I nearly went through with it, so I grabbed my razor and plunged it deep into my arms. I purposely cut myself. In my manic moods, I would think about returning to prostitution and the thought of it scared me so much that I had to stop myself. If I hurt myself so I couldn't work. I felt so distressed afterwards that I cried and cried. I called my parents, but they had nothing left to give. They were burned out from helping me. I spent two days in bed after that, crying. I hadn't cut myself in years. It had been a split second decision; I had to stop myself somehow from making critical decisions so compulsively.

Slowly, in the following weeks, I was strong enough to return to work at the retail shop, but things weren't the same. My store manager was so supportive and encouraging. The worst part was feeling I'd let him down; on my new medication, I could hardly concentrate. I still felt pressure from staring at the amount of cages I had to stock. My arm was sore from cutting, and I now felt like I was the 'bipolar girl'. I wanted to prove myself worthy again; that I could be a good employee.

My manager often stopped me and encouraged me with my job, yet I felt completely the opposite inside. I hated letting people down, but I figured out quickly it would be more of a let-down if I stayed.

One day, I randomly decided I didn't want to do this anymore. I couldn't try any longer. I was so tired of my ups and downs; I was so tired of trying. I turned to my manager and calmly explained this would be my last day.

I finished my shift and went home, and a weight lifted off my shoulders. The depression lifted for about a day and I was full of energy and excitement again, but it didn't last long.

Bipolar is cruel. Every time you have a good day, you believe it's working; you're well, you're stable, God is within reach, and your life is in control. But the next day it's a complete mind switch; everything's black, you cry for no reason, you fall flat on your face, and the most traumatising part of it is you believed you were finally getting better. It lies to you.

Visiting my family was hard; Mum and Dad just couldn't give any more to me. Although I didn't want to burden anyone else with my problems, I had two case managers that really came on board. They helped me by breaking down my day-to-day decisions; teaching me how to manage my everyday life.

I began meeting with them every day. I talked to them about the manic highs and the decisions I wanted to make. Then I would express my despair in my down times. They helped me to understand the complexities of my childhood and teenage trauma, and how it was all wrapped up in one big problem.

My brother and sister also became instrumental in my recovery during this time. I'd drop in and visit my brother and chat about my faith struggles; 'How come it has all turned out this way? How come God hasn't healed me like he once did?' He would empathise and often share his own struggles. Seeing his children and the love on their faces for me spurred me on to make good choices.

My sister and I started hanging out again. Going for walks and playing with her kids brought me such joy.

Slowly but surely, the medication kicked in, and my days felt peaceful again. It was like steering a ship; often I'd been aimless and lost at sea, but now I was heading towards the port. I ate proper meals, my sleep regulated, and I felt I could breathe again.

The hardest part, though, was that I had no vision or purpose for my life. I had no goals, apart from going for a walk every day. I found church hard, as it was always pushing you to be more like Jesus, but I felt barely alive as a Christian. I started small though; I began reading my Bible again.

During the times of darkness and despair, I just lay in my bed sobbing for God to heal me from bipolar, or asking him to end my life. It was devastating, looking back at how much I had changed. I had once been fit and active, happy, at peace with my family, and with lots of friends. Now, here I was burdening my family with this illness, isolating from my friends and barely able to stay through a church service. All I could see was a wrecked life.

One night I went to a church home-group. I was reluctant to go, but I knew making good choices was going to help me through. We watched a video message about stepping out in faith, believing for a better life. I felt angry and bitter. I'd stepped out in faith when I came off my medication. I believed that God had healed me.

After the video message, I told the group that I strongly disagreed with it, and how dangerous it was to listen to teachings like that. The group listened and understood as I shared about my journey with bipolar. I was surprised, though, when each one identified with what I was going through.

One lady had four miscarriages during her Christian walk. Each time she had believed God for a baby and then each time she lost it. She had cried out to God. 'Why had he forsaken her?' She'd spent a long time agonising over it, but she knew he loved and cared for her. She knew he would help her, and eventually she had given birth to a beautiful baby girl.

Another lady had spent years with broken teeth because of a genetic problem. All her teeth broke, and she couldn't afford to get them fixed. They made abscesses in her mouth and she'd had to syringe out the puss by herself. She prayed for years and suffered for years, asking for God to heal her. One day, a lady in her church gave her $4000 to fix her teeth. She declined at first, believing God would heal her, but then when she went home and asked God for healing he answered her, in her mind, and said "I'm trying!" So she went back and received the gift of money for new teeth. I can't imagine the pain and suffering she must have gone through for years. It must have affected her self-esteem and confidence and shaken her faith, but God came through.

It all resonated with me. Sometimes our sufferings feel as though God has abandoned us, but he hasn't. He is always there to comfort us. But what is the purpose of suffering?

In 2 Corinthians 1.3 I read, "*God comforts us in all our troubles, so that we can comfort others when they are troubled.*"

I began accepting my suffering, and as I did, I received a comforting peace within, that I knew came from God. He was steering my ship towards land. I was no longer aimless and out to sea.

One day I'll meet other people struggling with mental illness and my heart will break for them. I'll resonate with suffering and give empathy and comfort. Just like Jesus, I'll speak the truth about their situations. I can offer hope to the drug addicts because I have also climbed over the mountain of addiction. I have experienced instant healing from methamphetamine, but I also have experienced suffering where healing seems so far away. I have walked on both sides of the track; instant healing, and journeying through suffering.

So, there is hope for me! God comforts me, and one day I will comfort others. Suffering is not meaningless; you're never alone in your suffering. God is with you.

Now I am owned by God. He has adopted me. I am his, and although I may rise and fall, he is with me every step of the way, leading me into a life of peace.

Epilogue

It's a beautiful day. I've just been for a run, and now I'm snuggled back in bed with my Bible. This is my favourite time of the day. I'm so grateful for the ability to run. I'm now smoke free, drug free and happy.

My mood has balanced out with the medication, and relationships with my family are back on track. I visit my sister every Saturday and drop in to see my brother on the weekends. During the week, my parents are my greatest support and cheerleaders.

My case manager told me about a job opportunity as a peer support-worker for mental health and addictions. A prerequisite for the job was that you had to have had a mental illness or an addiction, to be hired. This was a miracle because, with my bipolar issues and counselling background, I could put to use my life experience and skills. I feel like everything I have been through now has a purpose.

I've been in this job for just over a year now, and I love it. I get to really help people, and my employers are such great supporters.

Life is good. I've found that a healthy diet, exercise, medication, family support and my faith have allowed me to stay well.

My purpose in sharing my story is so others may know there is hope.

I am free. You can be too.

Acknowledgements

I'd like to acknowledge God and thank him for giving me the inner strength to overcome life's challenges.

I'd like to thank my case managers, Bruce and Bernie, who walked beside me on this journey. I'd like to acknowledge their caring, non-judgmental approach, and their willingness to walk with me through the ups and the downs.

I'd like to thank my family for giving me a second chance and staying supportive when things got tough.

Also, I thank my two incredible friends, Guillaume and Benedict, who housed me through the roughest patch, and who let me sleep on their bedroom floor when I was paranoid.

I'd like to thank my employers, who took me back as a support worker; I love the job and am grateful for second chances.

I'd like to acknowledge my publisher, Jenny Jenkins, for believing in me and my story, and helping me to help others. This book wouldn't be possible if it weren't for her.

I want to acknowledge anyone who is reading this book and has had mental health or addiction problems; it's tough to break away from it all, but it's possible. Faith, fitness, and family are all things

I attribute to being well again. It started with a small walk around the block once a day, to now jogging and working out at the gym every other day. If you don't have good family support, find a local church and join a support group.

I acknowledge the identity associated with being unwell, but it's not who you are, and you can't let it define you. The Bible says, in 2 Corinthians 5.17: *'Anyone who belongs to Christ has become a new person. The old life has gone; a new life has begun!' (NLT)*

Finally, take courage and walk into freedom. It's more painful to stay owned by addiction and illness than it is to leave.

www.ingramcontent.com/pod-product-compliance
Lightning Source LLC
Chambersburg PA
CBHW072005290426
44109CB00018B/2138